# THE WAYS OF AN ATHEIST

## BERNARD KATZ

## Prometheus Books

59 John Glenn Drive
Amherst, New York 14228-2197

Published 1999 by Prometheus Books

03 02 01 00      5 4 3 2

Library of Congress Cataloging-in-Publication Data

Katz Bernard, 1924–.
   The ways of an atheist / by Bernard Katz.
      p.   cm.
   ISBN 1–57392–273–0 (alk. paper)
   1. Atheism. 2. Christianity—Controversial literature. 3. Religion—Controversial literature. I. Title.
BL2747.3.K294   1999
211´.8—dc21                                    98–47272
                                                                CIP

Printed in the United States of America on acid-free paper

# Contents

PREFACE                                                                 9

I.  WHAT ABOUT GOD?

    1. Made in the Image of God                                  15
    2. The Divine Seed                                            20
    3. What Is God Like?                                          22
    4. Is God Love?                                               23
    5. A Pagan's Objections to Christianity                       26
    6. The Argument from Design: The Latest Spin                  28

II.  WHOSE MORALITY?

    7. The Problem of Evil                                        33
    8. Biblical Ethics                                            36
    9. Religion: Breeder of Immorality                            38
  10. "Religion Is a Monumental Chapter
       in the History of Human Egotism"                          40
  11. Interpretation Is Everything                                 42
  12. Infallibility?                                               44

III.  MIRACLES AND MAGIC

  13. Are There Miracles?                                          49
  14. Were Miracles Important?                                     52
  15. The Magic Is the Same—Only the Techniques Have Changed       54

IV. RELIGION AND MENTAL ILLNESS

   16. Religion Is Injurious to Your Mental Health   59
   17. The Theological Roots of Arab Anti-Semitism   61
   18. Believe It or Not!   64

V. ARCHEOLOGY AND THE BIBLE

   19. The Spade Is Mightier Than the Word: Part 1   69
   20. The Spade Is Mightier Than the Word: Part 2   72
   21. The Spade Is Mightier Than the Word: Part 3   75
   22. Plagiarism or Research?   77

VI. JESUS: WARTS AND ALL

   23. The Devolution of Divine Revelation   81
   24. Suppose   83
   25. Capsule Arguments against Christ   85
   26. Was Jesus Mr. Nice Guy?   87
   27. Jesus the Sinner   89
   28. Jesus and the Ten Commandments: How Many Did He Break?   91
   29. The Fear and Cowardice of God   93
   30. Jesus and the Dagger Men   95
   31. Guess Who?   99

VII. THE MEANING OF CHRISTIAN SYMBOLS

   32. Twice-Born   103
   33. The Trinity   105
   34. The Fish Head   108

VIII. JEWS, CATHOLICS, AND FUNDAMENTALIST PROTESTANTS

   35. Monotheism: Breeder of Intolerance,
       Destruction, and Genocide   113
   36. Voltaire's Prayer   116
   37. Why Jews Don't Eat Pork   118
   38. Pious Lies   120
   39. Have the Fundamentalists Got It Wrong!   122
   40. A "Dear John" Letter to Creationists   125
   41. The Theological Sins of the Creationists   127
   42. Revelations about the Apocalypse and the Fundamentalists   130

IX. SCIENCE VERSUS RELIGION

   43. Monkeyshines at the Monkey Trial   135

44. The War Between Science and Religion          138
45. The Devil, Science!          141
46. Islam and Science          144

X. SECULAR HUMANISM

47. From Religious to Secular Literature:
    The Founding Fathers of Humanism          149

AFTERWORD          151

# Preface

For as long as I care to remember, religion—like the striptease—has always been a display of the power of suggestion. Like the Virgin Birth, it has all too often supported an immaculate deception.

As a boy, I remember the hypocrisy of Catholic schoolkids who, after peeling off like dive bombers from the end of the long line walking to church, disappeared into the local candy store to gamble at cards. Their church had little hold on them. I remember that at the height of the Great Depression, when folks hardly had enough to eat, a rabbi would travel to our community from Brooklyn to collect money for Yeshiva students. No doubt they felt it was more important to buttress rabbinical studies than to help those who had empty wallets and empty stomachs. Such experiences left a rotten taste in my mouth.

During my business life, I daily confronted the irrational. After all, I was a commodity and stockbroker who had worked a lifetime at making a living trading, say, pork belly futures and IBM. As such, I and my clients went through many boom and bust markets. These could not be explained until after the fact—and often not even then. Despite the fact that Jesus proclaimed that you can't worship both God and Mammon, my business wasn't hurt, even though most of my clients were Christians. So I concluded that I might learn something helpful by studying religion, an even more irrational area than the markets I traded in. I learned a great deal but, unfortunately, it didn't help.

Like a hound dog on the trail, I went wherever the scent took me. Nothing was too bloody, too bizarre, or too embarrassing to stop my investigation. Over fifty-plus years I've had to research just about every area pertaining to religion. In this book I've divided some of my findings into ten areas so as to give you a good taste of just how irrational and emotionally prone religion is. Although the chapters are based on solid scholarship, I wrote them so that an interested lay public would enjoy them.

9

Since what we mean by religion almost always involves some kind of deity, the first part of this book deals with ideas about God. These are grouped into two parts: revealed religion and natural religion. The first is anchored in what we read in the Bible and other sacred works; the second in philosophy. Books that I found very helpful are Lee Carter's *Lucifer's Handbook* (Academic Associates, 1977), Walter Kaufmann's *Critique of Religion and Philosophy* (Harper Torchbooks, 1958), and Al Seckel's (ed.) *Bertrand Russell on God and Religion* (Prometheus Books, 1986).

Because all religions of the West fail to explain the problem of evil, and since this is their worst Achilles' heel, I began part two with a hard-hitting examination of evil, combining this with an analysis of morality. Fundamentalists of all kinds, including important congressional politicians, want us—through legislation if necessary—to regain our alleged lost sense of morality by following the Bible. Here I've tried to demonstrate that this is impossible. An old favorite of mine is Joseph McCabe's *The Story of Religious Controversy*, edited by E. Haldeman-Julius (The Strafford Company, Pub., 1929).

"Miracles and Magic" is the title of the third part. Judaism, Christianity, and Islam are nourished by miracles and magic. Paganism—which these religions ridicule—has supplied many of the rituals and symbols Western religions now depend on. Without miracles and magic, they would soon starve to death. As you will see, these are just two names for the same nonsense. An excellent book, and one by a top gun in the secular humanist movement, is Morton Smith's *Jesus the Magician* (Barnes and Noble, 1978).

The fourth part is a reply to the current claims that religion is beneficial to your mental health. I maintain, instead, that there should be a warning label on every Bible that says "reading this may be injurious to your health." I've included a refutation to Islamic pretensions that, according to the Koran, all people are to be tolerated. Events for some centuries in Islamic countries prove otherwise. Many ask why Arabs are anti-Semitic even though they themselves are Semites. The answer is in the Koran. Franklin H. Littel's book *The Crucifixion of the Jews* (Harper and Row, 1975) combines an analysis of Christian anti-Semitism with that of Islam.

Part five, "Archaeology and the Bible," is devoted to dispelling the well-accepted myth that "the Bible proves history." You will find here that the spade has done more burying than enlightening.

Part six is an annihilation of the "Mr. Good Guy" image of Jesus Christ, including his so-called elevation to the godhead. After all, any attack on Christianity must include its progenitor! An excellent book in this area is Rudolph Augstein's *Jesus Son of Man* (Urizen Books, 1972).

Part seven, "The Meaning of Christian Symbols," demonstrates the utter dependency on pagan sexuality—its symbols, rituals, and their meanings. This part hits the underbelly of our religions. An excellent book in this regard is James Ballantyne Hanney's *The Rise and Fall of the Roman Empire* (self-published by the author in 1913 because of censorship by the British government). You probably can get it through interlibrary loan. Busenbark's *Symbols, Sex, and the Stars* (Truthseeker Co., 1949) is also outstanding.

The eighth part is a potpourri of very interesting and important comments about religion. "Why Jews Don't Eat Pork" is a theme that's been so perfumed that it's accepted by many intelligent Jews. Solomon Reinach, a fine French scholar, tells it like it is in his *Orpheus, A History of Religions* (Horace Liveright, 1930). This is one of the books Will and Ariel Durant depended on when they wrote their wonderful history series.

The ninth part deals with science and religion. Since our movement prides itself on using scientific method and the tentative findings of science, and since there has been a clash between science and religion ever since the age of Newton, I felt it necessary to explore this. One of the civil trials that mirrored this conflict was the Scopes "Monkey Trial" (1925) concerning the teaching of evolution in the classroom. There has been so much balderdash associated with this that I thought it would be novel and enlightening to get at the truth. It should startle you. My favorite reference is a two-book set by Andrew D. White, who wrote the American classic *A History of the Warfare of Science with Theology in Christendom*, (originally published by MacMillan and Co., 1896). For religion, this is the "poison pill."

The last part deals briefly with secular humanism. Two outstanding books I recommend here are: George H. Smith's *Atheism, the Case against God* (Prometheus Books, 1979), and Corliss Lamont's *The Philosophy of Humanism* (Frederick Ungar Pub., 1974).

Whether you speak or write, there is more than enough explosive material here to blow away any of our common enemy. Do not be afraid to use it.

# WHAT ABOUT GOD?

# 1

# Made in the Image of God

Then God said: "Let us make man in our image, after our likeness . . ." (Gen. 1:26).

To this day there is a great discussion as to what this means.

But there is no question as to its meaning. The passage makes it quite clear that we have the same characteristics as the God who created us. This is easily proven from scripture itself. Let us look at ourselves as we are reflected in the image of God.

## WE LIE—JUST AS GOD DID

"From the fruits of the trees in the garden we may eat," the woman said to the serpent; "it is only concerning the fruit of the tree which is in the middle of the garden that God has said, "You may not eat any of it, nor touch it, lest you die." But the serpent said to the woman, "You would not die at all; for God knows that the very day you eat it, your eyes will be opened, and you will be like gods who know good from evil" (Gen. 3:2–5).

We know that they did not die!

## WE PUNISH WITHOUT PROPER REASONS—JUST AS GOD DID

"In the course of time Cain brought some produce of the soil as an offering to the Lord, while Abel on his own part brought some firstlings from his flock, that is, some fat pieces from them. The Lord took notice of Abel and his offering; but of Cain and his offering he took no notice. So Cain became very angry and downcast. Then the Lord said to Cain, 'Why are you angry, and why are you downcast? If you have been doing right, should you not be happy? But if you have not, sin will be lurking at the door. And yet he is devoted to you, while you rule over him.'

"Then Cain said to his brother Abel, 'Let us go off into the country.'

"When they were out in the country, Cain attacked his brother Abel, and murdered him.

"Then the Lord said to Cain, 'Where is your brother Abel?'

" 'I do not know,' he said. 'Am I my brother's keeper?'

"Whereupon he said, 'What have you done? Hark, your brother's blood is crying to me from the ground! And now, cursed shall you be in banishment from the soil' " (Gen. 4:3–11).

How could Cain know what offering was pleasing to the Lord when the Lord had not informed him so? Again, how could Cain know he was committing a terrible crime when the Lord never instructed him so? Clearly, God punished unjustly!

## WE GIVE NO RATIONAL REASONS FOR OUR ACTIONS—JUST AS GOD DID

"Then God said, 'Let us make man in our image . . .' " (Gen. 1:26).

". . . God saw that all he had made was very good" (Gen. 1:31).

"[T]he Lord regretted that he had ever made man on the earth, and he grieved to the heart. So the Lord said, 'I will blot the men that I have created off the face of earth, both men and animals, reptiles, and the birds of the air; for I regret that I ever made them' " (Gen. 6:6–7).

God contradicted himself and in doing so acted irrationally. After he creates he congratulates himself by saying that everything was very good. Then when things get out of hand (his hand I might add), he changes his opinion of his own handiwork and destroys almost all of it.

## WE PLAY FAVORITES—JUST AS GOD DID

"In the course of time Cain brought some produce of the soil as an offering to the Lord, while Abel on his part brought some firstlings from his flock. . . . The Lord took notice of Abel and his offering; but of Cain and his offering he took no notice" (Gen. 4:3–6).

"Noah, however, found favor with the Lord" (Gen. 6:8).

If we are all God's children, why should he play favorites?

## WE CURSE THOSE WHO DISOBEY US—JUST AS GOD DID

"So the Lord said to the serpent, 'Because you have done this, the most cursed of all animals shall you be.'

"To the woman he said: 'I will make your pain at childbirth very great. . . .' And to the man he said, 'Because you followed your wife's suggestions, and ate from the tree from which I commanded you not to eat, cursed shall be the ground through you, in suffering shall you gain your living from it as long as you live . . .' " (Gen. 3:14–17).

"Whereupon God said to Cain, 'What have you done? Hark, your brother's blood is crying to me from the ground! And now, cursed shall you be in banishment from the soil . . . a vagrant and vagabond shall you be on earth' " (Gen. 4:10–12).

## WE TOLERATE DRUNKENNESS—JUST AS GOD DID

"Now Noah was the first farmer to plant a vineyard. Having drunk some of the wine, he became intoxicated, and lay uncovered in his tent." (Gen. 9:20–22)

If getting drunk is so terrible, why did God allow Noah to do so? After all, Noah and the men in his immediate family were the only ones on earth not blotted out, because "Noah, however, had found favor with the Lord." (Gen. 6:8)

## WE TOLERATE SLAVERY—JUST AS GOD DID

"When Noah awoke from his wine, and learned what his youngest son had done to him, he said, 'Cursed be Canaan! The meanest of slaves shall he be to his brothers.'

"Also he said, 'Blessed of the Lord may Shem be; and let Canaan be his slave! May God expand Japheth, and dwell in the tents of Shem; but let Canaan be his slave!' " (Gen. 9:24–27).

Such is one of the great rationalizations for the institution of slavery!

## WE ARE AFRAID OF THE ABILITY OF OTHERS—JUST AS GOD WAS

"Then the Lord came down to look at the city and tower which humans had built. The Lord said, 'They are just one people, and they all have the same language. If this is what they can do as a beginning, then nothing that they resolve to do will be impossible for them' " (Gen. 11:5–7).

Surely an all-powerful God should not be afraid of the puny efforts of man!

## WE HAVE DIFFICULTY WITH MATH—JUST AS GOD DID

"Then the Lord said, 'My spirit must not remain in man indefinitely, because it too will become flesh. Accordingly, his lifetime shall be one hundred and twenty years' " (Gen. 6:3).

"Noah lived altogether nine hundred and fifty years" (Gen. 9:29).

"Shem lived for five hundred years. . . .

Shelah lived four hundred and three years. . . .

Arpachshad lived four hundred and three years. . . .

Eber lived four hundred and thirty years. . . .

Peleg Lived two hundred and seven years. . . .

Reu lived two hundred and nine years. . . .

Serug lived two hundred years . . ." (Gen. 11:10–23).

## WE EVEN HAVE PHYSICAL CHARACTERISTICS—JUST LIKE GOD

"But when they heard the sound of God taking a walk in the garden for his daily airing . . ." (Gen. 3:8).

"Those that entered were a male and female of every kind of animal, as God had commanded him. Then the Lord shut him in" (Gen. 7:16).

"Then the Lord came down to look at the city and tower which human beings had built" (Gen. 11:5).

"The Lord appeared to him [Abraham] at the terebinth at Mamre. . . . Raising his eyes, he saw three men standing near him" (Gen. 18:1).

"The Lord spoke to Moses face to face, as one man would speak to another" (Exod. 33:11).

"However, the Lord said, 'Here is a place by me; station yourself on the rock; and when my glory passes by, I will put you in a cleft of the rock, and cover you with my hand until I pass by; then I will take away my hand, so that you may see my back, while my face shall not be seen" (Exod. 33:21–23).

## WE COMMIT ADULTERY AND FORNICATE—JUST AS GOD DID

"The Lord said to Abraham, 'Why is it that Sarah laughs, saying, 'Can I really bear a child when I am so old?' 'Is anything too wonderful for the Lord? I will come back to you at the appointed time, at the time for life to appear, and Sarah shall have a son' " (Gen. 18:13–14).

"The Lord dealt with Sarah, as he had said; and the Lord did to Sarah as he had promised. Sarah conceived, and at the time that God had indicated, she bore Abraham a son in his old age" (Gen. 21:1–2).

"When the Lord saw that Leah was slighted, he made her pregnant, while Rachel remained barren. So Leah conceived and bore a son. . . . 'For,' she said, 'the Lord has taken note of my distress; now my husband will love me' " (Gen.

29: 20–35). (She bore three more sons by the Lord: Simeon, Levi, and Judah. The first son by the Lord was named Rueben.)

"Now there was a certain man of Zorah. . . . whose name was Manoah. His wife was barren and childless; but the angel of the Lord appeared to the woman, and said to her, 'See now, although you have been barren and childless, you are going to conceive, and bear a son.' So the woman bore a son, and called his name Samson." (Judg. 13:2–4, 24)

"The birth of Jesus Christ came about thus. His mother Mary was betrothed to Joseph, but before they came together she was discovered to be pregnant by the Holy Ghost . . . [A]n angel of the Lord [appeared] to him in a dream, saying, 'Joseph . . . fear not to take Mary your wife home, for what is begotten in her comes from the Holy Ghost' " (Matt. 1:18–20).

"Let us make man in our image" had two important meanings for the authors of these verses and their audiences. They not only presupposed the presence of other gods, but they also conceived of God as being in the form of a human being. We are indeed like the God who created us!

# 2

# The Divine Seed

"No child of God commits sin, because the divine seed remains in him; indeed because he is God's child he cannot sin" (1 John 3:9).

Is this reference to "the divine seed [that] remains in him" to the physical semen from God's own material substance? Or should it be interpreted in a nonmaterial way—in a spiritual, poetical, or allegorical imagery? Did those who wrote both Testaments believe that God had used his own semen in the same way human males do?

The answer is yes.

Read what St. Paul says in Gal. 4:22: "For it is written, that Abraham had two sons, one by a bondmaid, the other by a free woman," and then examine the following texts in Genesis to which Paul refers.

"About this time next year I shall come back to you, and your wife Sarah will have a son." Now Sarah was standing and listening at the opening of the tent close by him. Both Abraham and Sarah were very old, Sarah being well past the age of childbearing. So she laughed to herself and said, 'At my time of life I am past bearing children, and my husband is old.' The Lord said to Abraham, 'Why did Sarah laugh and say, 'Can I really bear a child now that I'm so old?' Is anything impossible for the Lord? In due season, at this time next year, I shall come back to you, and Sarah shall have a son" (Gen. 18:10–14).

Skipping to Gen. 21:1–2, we see that God did impregnate Sarah: "The Lord showed favor to Sarah as he had promised, and made good what he had said about her. She conceived and at the time foretold by God she bore a son to Abraham in his old age."

This is not the only text that tells us that God literally impregnated women. Here's another:

"And Eli blessed Elkanah and his wife, and said, 'The Lord grant you children by this woman' . . . The Lord showed his care for Hannah, and she conceived and gave birth to three sons and two daughters" (1 Sam. 2:20–21).

The original Isaac cycle survived in Christian mythology. Jesus derives his human messianic office from his father, Joseph, but his divine essence comes from his divine Father through God's divine seed—just as Isaac was born from the implantation of holy seed. The truth of this is that the tradition of the Church connects the sacrifice of Isaac with that of Jesus. Parallels are to be found among most of the ancient civilizations, from the waters of the holy Indus river to the sacred Nile.

Because the Lord used his own seed to impregnate women, we may conclude at least two things: that the reference in 1 John 3:9 is to actual, physical seed from God himself, and that for that very reason we can state that we "were made in God's image."

# 3

# What Is God Like?

Hey there, have I got good news for you! I've just hit the jackpot. I've finally found out what God is like. And from an unimpeachable source too—the *Catholic Almanac.*

Here is what the Roman Catholic Church says: "God is: almighty, eternal, holy, immortal, immense, immutable, incomprehensible, ineffable, infinite, invisible, just, loving, merciful, most high, most wise, omnipotent, omniscient, omnipresent, patient, perfect, provident, supreme, true."

Was this the key to knowing God? Take the adjective "incomprehensible." The word means unintelligible, unfathomable. In turn, this means that since God is *unintelligible,* then Roman Catholics are *agnostics*! It also follows that none of the other characteristics can be known.

Many of these other terms are self-contradictory or contradict one another. "Immutable" means without change. Yet God is "loving" and "merciful," two adjectives that imply change. "Ineffable" means "indescribable." Yet there are all those descriptive adjectives.

Let's look at these descriptions another way—by putting them in a negative mode. "Infinite" is without limits. "Invisible" means not visible. "Eternal" means not subject to time. Apparently, Roman Catholics forget that negative concepts can only describe what is *not*—thereby making their God nonexistent! And words such as "just," "loving," "wise," and "merciful" are applicable only to humans.

So according to the *Catholic Almanac*'s authoritative definition, God is either human, unknowable, impossible, or nonexistent.

After this exercise, I was glad to be so enlightened. There are now three things I won't believe: how a guy got a black eye, how a gal got a mink coat, and how the Roman Catholics define God!

# 4

# Is God Love?

We are told constantly that God is love. We often see hanging from upper bleachers during a ball game a banner which says "John 3:16," which, if you look it up, says the same thing. In the sacred writings of the Jews we find this lofty spiritual concept in Deut. 6:5 and Hos. 14:5.

To see if this is true, let us examine a representative sampling of passages from both Testaments:

1. God so loved us that he created every living entity, declaring it was "good" (Gen. 1:21–22). Of course this included man-eating animals, fish, bacteria, and viruses.

2. God so loved us that he wiped all living things off the face of the earth except Noah and his family and that which was preserved in the ark (Gen. 6).

3. God so loved us that he killed the first-born of the Egyptians (Exod. 12:29).

4. God so loved us that he sanctioned slavery (Exod. 21:2–3).

5. God so loved us that he ordered slave-raiding parties (Deut. 20:10–15).

6. God so loved us that he sanctioned the capture and deflowering of women, after which they could be thrown aside (Deut. 10–14).

7. God so loved us that he commanded the killing of those who were supposed to be witches (Exod. 22:18).

8. God so loved us that he that he commanded the killing of those who were supposed to be wizards (Lev. 20:6).

9. God so loved us that he ordered the death of anyone who did not worship him only (Exod. 22:20).

10. God so loved us that he ordered death for anyone who practiced bestiality (Exod. 22:19).

11. God so loved us that he ordered death for anyone in a family who had a different religion, that is, worshiped other gods (Deut. 13:6–11).

12. God so loved us that he commanded death to any sabbath-breaker (Exod. 13:14–15).

13. God so loved us that he commanded that any uncircumcised male was to be outlawed from his kinfolk (Gen. 7:14).

14. God so loved us that he sanctioned death to anyone who blasphemed (Lev. 24:10–16).

15. God so loved us that he ordered death for any man caught having sex with a married woman, as well death for the woman herself (Deut. 22:22).

16. God so loved us that he ordered both men and women to be outlawed from their kinfolk if the man had intercourse with the woman during her monthly period (Lev. 20:18).

17. God so loved us that he answered complaints by sending poisonous snakes which killed many (Num. 21:5–6).

18. God so loved us that he ordered the massacre of a whole nation (Deut. 2:34).

19. God so loved us that he ordered a pestilence which killed seventy thousand people because David had sinned by taking a census (2 Sam. 24:15).

20. God so loved us that he himself killed 102 men just to prove that Elijah was a true prophet (1 Kings 1:10–12).

21. God so loved us that he commanded vengeance upon the fourth generation of children for the sins of their fathers (Num. 14:8).

22. God so loved us that these very commands were to be continued by the followers of Jesus Christ (Matt. 5:17–19).

23. God so loved us that he promised eternal torment (Matt. 18:8; 25:41, 46).

24. God so loved us that he commanded all worshipers of the Devil to suffer eternal torment (Rev. 14:9–11).

25. God so loved us that he condemned us all to torment because of our inheritance of the sin of Adam (Rom. 5:18). Since this goes way beyond the fourth generation as described in number 21, it is evident that God changed his mind.

26. God so loved us that he commanded that the great majority of mankind will go to hell (Matt. 7:13–14).

27. God so loved us that he condemned to everlasting destruction those who do not know the Father or his Son's Gospel (2 Thess. 1:7–9).

28. God so loved us that he condemned to hellfire those of us who call others fools (Matt. 5:22).

29. God so loved us that he damned anyone who does not believe in his Son (John 3:36).

30. God so loved us that he damned those who were rich (Luke 6:24).

31. God so loved us that he damned even those who are well-spoken of (Luke 6:26).

32. God so loved us that he allowed devils to possess men (Matt. 8:16).

33. God so loved us that he sacrificed an innocent person for our sins (1 Pet. 2:24; Heb. 9:26).

34. God so loved us that he required the death of an only Son as a victim before he could relinquish his vengeance on sinners whom he had made imperfect in the first place (John 3:16; 1 John 4:10).

35. God so loved us that he sacrificed his only Son to redeem us from the curse of the very same law which he commanded us to obey in the first place (Gal. 3:13).

36. God so loved us that he actually sent delusions to entrap us into being damned (2 Thess. 2:11–12).

37. God so loved us that he actually hardened people's hearts so that they would not be saved from hell (John 12:39–40).

38. God so loved us that it is impossible for any man to save himself by his own will and efforts from hell, for God has already chosen those he will save (Rom. 9:11–16; Eph. 1:4).

39. God so loved us that he allowed his elect to do anything immoral (Rom. 8:33–34).

40. God so loved us that he allowed us to eat him (John 6:53–56).

Think. Is God love?

# 5

# A Pagan's Objections to Christianity

Many people know very little about what pagans said about the upstart Christians. This is because the Church destroyed as many objectional commentaries as possible. As a result most of what we know came from the rebuttals Christians made to the pagan arguments. Fortunately, we have such a source from one of the geniuses of the ancient Church, a philosopher and teacher from Alexandria, Egypt, named Origen.

This leading churchman wrote a lengthy rebuttal to Christianity's "first great polemical adversary," a foremost pagan philosopher named Celsus. In his *Contra Celsum* we have a great many quotations from Celsus which bring out clearly the line of Celsus's arguments against Christianity. The work that Origen attacked was titled *True Discourse* and was written about 177 C.E. What follows is a long quotation from Celsus as he is quoted by Origen.

> Their [the Christians'] injunctions are like this: "Let no one educated, no one wise, no one sensible draw near. For these abilities are thought by us to be evils. But as for anyone ignorant, anyone stupid, anyone uneducated, anyone who is a child, let him come boldly." By the fact that they themselves admit that these people are worthy of the God, they show that they want and are able to convince only the foolish, dishonorable and stupid, and only slaves, women, and little children. . . . Moreover, we see that those who display their trickery in the market-places and go about begging would never enter a gathering of intelligent men, nor would they dare to reveal their noble beliefs in their presence; but whenever they see adolescent boys and a crowd of slaves and a company of fools they push themselves in and show off. . . . In private houses also we see wool-workers, cobblers, laundry-workers, and the most illiterate and bucolic yokels, who would not dare to say anything at all in front of their elders and more intelligent masters. But whenever they get hold of children in private and some stupid women with them, they let out some astounding statements as, for

example, that they must not pay any attention to their father and school-teacher, but must obey them [the Christians]; they say that these [their fathers and teachers] talk nonsense and have no understanding, and that in reality they neither know nor are able to do anything good, but are taken up with mere empty chatter. But they alone [the Christians], they say, know the right way to live, and if the children would believe them, they would become happy and make their home happy as well. And if just as they are speaking they see one of the school-teachers coming, or some intelligent person, or even the father himself, the more cautious of them flee in all directions; but the more reckless urge the children on to rebel. They whisper to them that in the presence of their father and schoolmasters they do not feel able to explain to the children anything, since they do not want to have anything to do with the silly and obtuse teachers who are totally corrupted and far gone in wickedness and who inflict punishment on the children. But, if they like, they should leave father and their schoolmasters, and go along with the women and little children who are their play-fellows to the wooldresser's shop, or to the cobbler's or the washer woman's shop, that they may learn perfection. And by saying this they persuade them.[1]

Don't you get the feeling that Celsus was the progenitor of secular humanism? He puts forth the very same arguments we moderns do, including such liberal Christians as John Shelby Spong the Episcopal bishop of Newark, New Jersey: the Church's teachings were offered most often to the great unwashed—the unsophisticated and uneducated, a public unable to tell truth from nonsense, to children, slaves, and mostly women—by people of low standing in the community. We should all include the pagan Celsus in our roster of those worthy of emulation.

NOTE

1. Quoted in Ramsey Macmullen, *Christianizing the Roman Empire, A.D. 100–400* (New Haven: Yale University Press, 1984), pp. 37 ff.

# 6

# The Argument from Design: The Latest Spin

In order to prove there is a God, two types of arguments have been developed: one is called revealed religion and is based on the Bible; the other is natural religion and is based on intellectual or philosophical arguments. Natural religion includes the argument from design—which is the basis for this essay— and it in turn falls under what is called the "teleological argument." You would have thought that with all the heavy guns that have been trained on these ersatz arguments over the years, the intellectual firepower would have blown them to kingdom come. But no such luck.

As Jesus was supposedly resurrected, so has been the argument from design —only this time with a different spin. Michael J. Behe, professor of biochemistry at Lehigh University in Bethlehem, Pennsylvania, and loyal son of the Catholic Church, has written a book, *Darwin's Black Box: The Biochemical Challenge to Evolution.* It was chosen the "Book of the Year" in 1996 by that unimpeachable authority, the publishers of the evangelical magazine *Christianity Today.*

Now for some background.

The argument from design holds that nature is orderly: the planets move in regular orbits, planted seeds grow uniformly into complex structures, the seasons succeed each other in order. Everything conforms to patterns, is governed by law. This gigantic order of nature cannot have ordered it itself in this way, nor can it have been a huge accident. It requires the existence of an intelligence who was responsible for it. The presence of a pattern or structure requires that we assume an architect or *designer* who did this.

Apparently Aristotle originated the argument from design. Taking their cues from him, Augustine and Thomas Aquinas converted the argument to benefit Christianity. Here's how Thomas Aquinas put it: "As the arrow is directed by the archer, so the world is directed by an intelligent being."

Hume probed the argument with his analytical eye, pointing out that the teleological or design argument, given the nature of the world, could at best prove only a finite, imperfect deity—one that was wholly at odds with the Christian idea of a Trinitarian God.

In his analysis of these same philosophical arguments, Kant also concluded that the teleological argument was invalid.

And Darwin himself did not buy into the argument from design, but assigned species changes to natural causes. He would not have accepted the corollary advanced by believers that the theory of evolution proves that the world's progressive development is due to the underlying direction and purpose of a designer.

This brings us to the "black box." A black box is any device that functions perfectly well but whose inner workings remain mysterious, either because they cannot be seen or because they cannot be understood. For Charles Darwin, writing in the 1850s, the cell was the black box because microscopy hadn't advanced far, preventing Darwin from seeing the cell or understanding it. He thought the cell was a simple, undifferentiated blob of protoplasm.

We now know that Darwin was wrong about the cell. The cell is anything but simple. In fact, it's so different from what Darwin believed that Behe set his whole argument from design on its complexity. It is, Behe writes, "an irreducibly complex system . . . composed of several well-matched, interacting parts that contribute to the basic function, wherein the removal of any one of these parts causes the system to effectively cease functioning."

And here's where Behe uses verbal jujitsu, turning Darwin's admissions against him. For in *The Origin of the Species,* Darwin himself had noted that "if it could be demonstrated that any complex organ existed which could not possibly have been formed by numerous, successive, slight modifications, my theory would absolutely break down."

According to Behe, this is Darwin's Achilles' heel. Darwin runs into trouble in explaining macroevolution, or "large changes that seem to require coordination. An example is the development of flight in birds or the development of feathers." The Darwinian explanation of such larger changes, Behe points out, rests on two premises: natural selection—the famous "survival of the fittest"—and random variation, the notion that every evolutionary change was a chance occurrence. It is the latter premise that we atheists and nonbelievers accept—and that Behe challenges.

"In the past half-century," explains Behe, "we have discovered such intricacy, precision and such mind-boggling devices and processes that a number of scientists have seen these as an implication for design in the universe."

Behe is opposed by other Christians, among whom is Terry M. Gray, a biochemist who is a computer support scientist in the chemistry department at Colorado State University. Gray, a conservative Presbyterian, uses the same argument that has always been used to refute this viewpoint—namely, that further research may well explain the mystery of irreducible complexity. Simply because we do not know everything is no reason to believe that what *appears* to have been designed must necessarily be the result of supernatural forces.

Gray also has theological concerns. Gray said that Behe's model of an unevolving cell implies an interruption of God's normal operation of being constantly involved. He believes that the universe is maintained by God himself in day-by-day, minute-by-minute, second-by-second operations, not in the hands-off, clock-maker way suggested by deists.

In the meantime, Gray admits, "There are a lot of comparative studies serving to support the evolution hypotheses."

It should be added that entomologist Richard Dawkins, a strong advocate of a strictly nonreligious, materialistic interpretation of biological change, defines biology as "the study of complicated things that give the *appearance* of having been designed for a purpose" (italics mine).

Behe hasn't been afraid to go out on the limb, but I'm afraid that the fruit he finds there is poisoned.

# WHOSE MORALITY?

# 7

# The Problem of Evil

Except for the problem of evil, there would be little need for religion. The evils which afflict man and those he commits himself (sin) have been the grand theme and province of religion. The book of Job, a literary masterpiece, explores this problem of theodicy but, from a rational point of view, no satisfactory answer is supplied. What have been some of the other explanations of the origin of evil and its meaning?

1. There are two gods, one who is good and beneficent, and another who is evil and malevolent. This is the solution offered by Zoroastrianism, the Gnostics, Manichaeanism, and many of the original Christian churches.

That this dualism was and is still part of Christianity can be found in the text in the New Testament: in John 8:44 where Jesus accuses the Jews: "You are of your father the devil"; in Matt. 13:38: "The field is the world; the good seed are the children of the kingdom, but the tares are the children of the wicked one"; and in 1 John 3:8: "He that commits sin is of the devil. . . ."

Such a solution is untenable because it denies the monotheism of God so dearly protected and exclaimed by the Western religions. To avoid impaling itself on the horns of this dilemma, the Old Testament proclaims that God is the cause of *both* good and evil (Amos 3:6; Isa. 45:7).

But this does not avoid the other horn. By maintaining this consistency, it follows that God is not all-good. And that, of course, makes this solution completely unacceptable.

2. Instead of projecting two gods, the evil force (called the Devil) operates in heaven and in this world by the leave, as it were, of the one God. God himself created this rebellious evil being and all his followers who affect the spiritual and material worlds. The Devil and his host of followers has been a persistent theme in the Judeo-Christian tradition.

But a literal belief in the Devil does not absolve God of the problem of

33

evil—it simply adds to it. Why does God allow this great evil to exist and to destroy while all along God is supposed to be constructive? Once again, this leads to an unsatisfactory solution, for God is not all-good.

3. An extension of the above deals with the factor of "freedom." Apparently the Devil and his followers have this "freedom" to do evil. This freedom extends to all of nature, from the simplest atom to that of the most complex organism, man. The myth of the fall of man now includes the fall of all creation; that is, evil motivation exists along with the constructive purpose in the physical order. This, too, has a biblical basis: "They have made it desolate, and being desolate it mourns for me" (Jer. 12:11); and "For we know that the whole creation has been groaning in travail until now; not only the creation, but we ourselves . . ." (Rom. 8:22–23). But if we assume that the material order is operating with "freedom," God as the creator of the physical order is still left as being the source of the evil and, therefore, is not all good.

4. There is only one God whose motives are a mixture of good and evil, as in the case of man, and demonstrated in the Old Testament under explanation 1 above. But this contradicts the belief in a God who is all good, since this goodness has been supposedly demonstrated to the satisfaction of the Christians in the life, teachings, sacrificial death, and victorious resurrection of Jesus Christ. It also flies in the face of the Jews and Muslims, who worship God as an Absolute among whose characteristics is that he is all good.

5. This leads to the doctrine of predestination: before all worlds were created, a limited number of men yet to be created were elected to salvation and are predestined, willy-nilly, to eternal bliss, while the rest of mankind has been predestined to eternal damnation. It is further claimed that the good things in the life of the elect, and the evil things of the damned, are the predestined outcome of their unearned status before God.

This doctrine is clearly brought out by Paul: "When he did predestinate, them he called: and whom he called, them he also justified: and whom he justified, them he also glorified" (Rom. 8:30). But this doctrine is merely a wrinkle of explanations 1 and 4, above. What it comes down to in the end is that God deliberately and effectively wills an evil outcome for the mass of mankind and, therefore, while God is all-powerful, he is not all good.

6. Another attempt out of this dilemma is to structure one God who is all-good but not all-powerful. He would like things to go better, but he is not quite on top of them. This view can be conceived in a number of ways: (a) God never was and never will be all-powerful; (b) God himself is part of the evolutionary process and has not yet fully evolved into absolute power; and (c) in the evolution of matter, God's dynamic energy is confronted with a high degree of inertness in the material universe, thereby requiring time for things to shape up.

But (a) is totally at odds with the oneness of God as the Ultimate Ground of Being, for it leaves him merely as one being besides other beings.

The assumptions (a) and (b) are also unsatisfactory because they imply a continuing progress in the ordering of the universe, and our experience has been that this is not at all empirically evident. (Are the evils from hurricanes and earth-quakes less frequent now than they have been in past centuries?) On the other hand, the evolution of higher animals and man does indicate a progressive ordering of some parts of the universe. Yet at the same time animals and men are the causes of new evils.

7. Another theory is that there is one God, all-powerful and basically good, but who literally brings evil upon us. This is the same argument as in explanation 1 above, the difference being that God brings evil upon us in order to punish us. Although there is considerable biblical precedent for this theory, it is implausible for a number of reasons.

The first is that the degree of evil often seems to be disproportionate to the offense. After all, we expect God to be at least as just as an informed judge who hands out a sentence to fit the crime.

The second is that there is no obvious correlation between the sinners and the recipients of evil. This is brought out in Psalms 10 and 13 and in John 9:1–3.

And the third is that the means of punishment is not proper. Because children were making fun of the prophet Elisha, calling him a "baldhead," he cursed them in the name of God, after which two bears came out of the woods and mangled forty-two of the boys. If we do not expect parents to punish in this extreme way, certainly God should not!

8. The last theory is a modification of explanations 1 and 7. There is one God who is all-powerful and basically good, but he deliberately brings evil upon us to test us so that we may develop faith and trust in him.

This, too, has a biblical basis: "My son, do not despise the discipline of the Lord, nor faint when you are rebuked by him: For whom the Lord loves he chastens, and scourges every son whom he receives" (Heb. 12:5–6).

Again, we expect more of God than of a good parent (see Matt. 7:9–11). An earthly father would not deliberately inflict pain in order to test his child to see whether he can "take it."

From a rationalist point of view, none of the eight theories answers the problem of evil. Neither religion, nor its apologists, nor its theologians have ever answered the question "Whence and why evil?"

# 8

# Biblical Ethics

With the Bible to be taken literally and all its contents inspired by God as their creed, Christian Fundamentalists are on a political rampage trying to shove their brand of ethical medicine down our throats as their cure for what ails us. Are they right in their dogmatic approach to ethics? Absolutely not! For there is no question that there are more than enough passages in the Old Testament which are, from our modern point of view, quite immoral. This has been attested by overwhelming numbers of commentators, atheistic as well as fervent Jewish and Christian analysts.

Just to show you some of these horrors, here are a few scriptural reminders:

1. You shall not allow any sorceress to live (Exod. 22:18).

2. Whoever lies with a beast shall be put to death (Exod. 22:19).

3. Whoever sacrifices to any god, except the Lord alone, he shall be solemnly destroyed (Exod. 22:20).

4. Keep the sabbath; it is a sacred day for you, and anyone who desecrates it shall be put to death (Exod. 31:14).

5. Any man or woman who is a medium or a wizard must be put to death (Lev. 20:27).

6. As for that prophet or dreamer, he shall be put to death for his talk of apostasy from your God (Deut. 13:5).

7. If you hear that in any towns which the Lord your God has given you to stay in, some low creatures have . . . allured their fellow citizens with the cry, "Let us go and worship other gods . . . you must slay . . . the cattle and human beings alike" (Deut. 13:12–15).

8. When you set out to war . . . and take prisoners . . . if you see a beautiful woman whom you desire and long to marry, take her home . . . then you can have intercourse with her and be her husband, and she shall be your wife. After that, if you do not care for her, let her go where she pleases (Deut. 21:10–14).

Had enough "x-rated" texts? There are more than enough additional purple passages to please any bloodthirsty religionist. What is not well known, however, is that the Bible itself provides its own witnesses against the dogmatic interpretation of the Fundamentalists. These erring and misguided Christians should reexamine some of the Old Testament prophets, for they commented adversely on what had been accepted even in their days as divine authority. Take Jeremiah for instance. He is negating the plain meaning of Exod. 20:5 which states "for I . . . your God, am a jealous God, punishing the children for the sins of their fathers . . . down to the third and fourth generation." Jeremiah is so displeased with this extended punishment that he makes a new law: "Then they shall say no more, 'The fathers ate sour grapes, and the children's teeth are on edge'; but each shall die for his own sin, and he who eats the sour grapes, his own teeth shall be set on edge" (Jer. 31:29–30).

Ezekiel mirrors Jeremiah: "By my life! says the Lord God, you must never quote that proverb again in Israel" (Ezek. 18:1–4).

Ezekiel then follows this up by an overall indictment which comes from his Lord: "And I said to their children in the wilderness, do not walk in the statutes of your fathers, nor observe their ordinances" (20:18). Then the prophet lets the cat out of the bag, for he admits that his God "gave them statutes that were not good and ordinances by which they could not have life" (20:25). It's obvious that, according to Ezekiel, these death-dealing commandments had to be overthrown!

Jeremiah also makes it crystal clear that the scribes have "doctored up" the laws, saying: "How can you say, 'We are wise, and the word of the Lord is with us?' But, behold, the false pen of the scribes has made it into a lie" (8:8).

Isaiah likewise is fulminating against prophets whose lies have led the people astray (9:15–16).

Thus many of the prophets recognized that there were laws which were lies, and which therefore had to be eliminated or modified to prevent the old atrocities from being repeated and to compel a more up-to-date morality better suited to the times and circumstances.

Just as the Old Testament witnesses against a dogmatic morality, so does the New Testament. For following in the footsteps of the older prophets was, in the eyes of the new Christian communities, the prophet par excellence, Jesus Christ. He also, but on his own authority, tells his devotees that the Mosaic legislation was imperfect. If these religious zealots and ignoramuses would restudy the fifth chapter of Matthew, they would discover that Jesus modifies and changes a number of the laws of Moses in his Sermon on the Mount. Their master also does this regarding clean and unclean food (Matt. 15:10–11) as well as revaluing the sabbath (Matt. 12:1–13).

Had men always remembered that the "divine commandments" were to be altered and even abolished as circumstances and the times demanded—and as recognized and done by the biblical witnesses themselves—then the cruelties inflicted in the name of their god would not have disgraced and made abhorrent religions in general and dogmatic Christianity in particular.

# 9

# Religion:
# Breeder of Immorality

A side from the bloody tragedies which religion has so often inflicted upon humanity, we are told over and over again by the Moral Majority that there can be no morals without religion. Goodness and religion, they say, are the Bobbsey twins of God.

If we judge theological opinions by their effects, however, we could be right in assuming that all morality is perfectly compatible with religion. "Be at-one-ment with God. Do as God has told you in the good Book," we are constantly admonished—from the pulpit of the one-room clapboard church to the pulpit in the new electronic church studio. The religious propaganda swirls from all the nooks and crannies of American society—from the weather-beaten storefronts on skid row to the sumptuous estates on Main Line, from the grass plots of little league baseball to the swank locker rooms of big league football. Ah, what morals we would have if we would only imitate God!

But which God shall we pattern ourselves on, Yahweh of the Jews or Jesus of the Christians?

A few snatches from the Psalms are all we need to jar us back to the reality as to how we should behave if we follow Yahweh:

'Twas he who killed the first-born within Egypt,
both of man and beast,
who sent portents upon Egypt. . . .
many a nation he struck down,
and mighty kings he slew. . . . (Psalm 135:8–10)

The Edomites! remember
against them, Eternal,
that day of Jerusalem's fall,
when "Down with her! down with her!"

Edomites cried,
"Raze her to the ground!"
And you, Babylonians, you who plundered us,
a blessing on him who deals to you
all that you have dealt to us!
A blessing on him who snatches
your babes
and dashes them down on the rocks! (Psalm 137:7–9)

A great couple of poems, let us say, full of pathos and beauty, but also of savagery which any Apache might with equal justification have uttered.

Do we want to be as savage as the Old Testament God, raging, vengeful, slaughtering babes! There's no morality here!

Shall we, then, imitate the Jesus of the Christians? This God triumphed, claim his devotees, over other gods because he alone seemed to offer success through failure, dying to appease the implacable fury of his Father, Yahweh. This is not in the cards either. We will see in Jesus nothing but a fanatic preaching to the poor to stay poor—for won't they inherit the earth?—to hate pleasure, to seek suffering. Jesus says to leave your father and mother if you want to follow him (Luke 14:26). If you can, Jesus recommended that you make yourself a eunuch for the sake of the kingdom of Heaven (Matt. 19:12). With this in mind Origen, the great Church Father, castrated himself. Is this a proper morality for us, or is it for a member of the Sistine choir or some monastic order? Do not such morals tell us more about Jesus—or the aberrations of his so-called biographers and early followers—than give us the practical guidance we need?

If God has created everything for the use of his creatures, as we are assured in the first chapter of Genesis, by what strange caprice does he forbid the use of good things? Is the pleasure which man constantly desires but a snare that God has maliciously laid in his path to entrap him? The coincidence between Babylonian-Jewish-Christian morality and the inhumanity of this century is not accidental. It is inherent in the frame of mind that elevates spirituality at the expense of humanity. In one sense the Moral Majority is perfectly correct. There certainly is a connection between morality and religion—religion breeds immorality!

# 10

# "Religion Is a Monumental Chapter in the History of Human Egotism"

—William James

What is deity but the projection of ourselves and of nature? This is most easily brought out by the vast number of different gods and goddesses worshiped by the ancients. Their spirits incarnated the gamut of human emotions, thought, and behavior. There were the nature gods of the sun, moon, and rain, to name a few. We find family gods of the door, the well, and the hearth. Worshiped were the gods of peace, war, purity, and love. Our ancestors—people who were great in war, heroes, and outstanding emperors and kings—were made into gods. Supreme personal gods were Yahweh of Israel, the Father, Son, Holy Ghost, and Devil of the Christians, and Allah of Islam. Representing the sexual divinities were the male fertility gods, the mother goddesses, and their sons and consorts.

If you were to bet that all the nature and pagan gods are now gone, you would lose big. Some that you thought were dead and gone are very much alive. The "death of God" concept so much in the limelight a few generations ago has itself become dead and buried. Proof is the recent visit of a "living goddess" from India.

In the lush Hindu cosmology, Brahma is the creator and the source of all knowledge. His consort, the goddess Saraswati, is a fertile, life-giving mother. Today her spirit and incarnation live on in an Indian woman, Karunamayi Bhagavati. Her devotees have regarded her from her birth as the living incarnation of Saraswati. Believers say her divine birth in 1959 was prophesied by the "silent one," Ramani Haharishi, and that she left home at the age of twenty-one for a remote South Indian forest where she meditated for ten years before emerging with a mission to spread her message of peace and compassion around the world. The "Beloved Mother" was making her fourth trip to the United States to give a series of talks about meditation mantras and healing mantras.

Not all Hindus accept this specific incarnation, and there is no authoritative method for assessing her claim. Still, Hindus do believe that God can take many human forms. In India, when a "saint" appears to be merged in the "supreme reality" (that's their terminology, not mine), they say that even though the saint seems to be limited like the rest of mankind, her essence is one with God and, therefore, the saint is God. Another saint put it succinctly: "The truth is we are all incarnations of God; it's just that saints know they are."

Linda Johnson asks and answers this question in her book *Mother Teresa: Protector of the Sick* (Blackbirch Pub., 1997). She says: "In India, it is more difficult for articulate but egotistical speakers to set themselves up as gurus. With thousands of years experience, Indians can tell when it is the Mother's radiance shining through a human frame, and when it is Mahisha's, who is the shape-shifting demon of self-aggrandizement." What blarney, or whatever a nonbelieving Hindu would say! You can drive the popemobile through the holes in this rationalization.

In this, I'm on the side of William James's appraisal that "religion is a monumental chapter in the history of human egotism." I'm afraid that I would not qualify for Hindu sainthood. Not only don't I believe that I am God, I don't even know what that means!

# 11

# Interpretation Is Everything

Fundamentalist Christians keep saying that all the rules and morality needed for the good life are in the Bible. No one has to read any Miss Lovelorn column or the Boy Scout Manual to know what to do. No, sir, the Bible has all the answers! Even President Reagan stood four square on this. Are they right?

One of the best ways to evaluate this is to see what the people who wrote the Bible thought and did. If you read the Old Testament you will soon see that too many of the moral injunctions of the Bible are written too broadly—much more detail is needed. The Jews also found this out. They were forced to expand all the time on the generalities and hints they read in their Torah. Much of this extra commentary has been captured in what is known as the Talmudic literature. This is a vast literature accumulated over hundreds of years of study and fierce arguments by seventeen generations of rabbis. The arguments were mostly about points of religious law and ethics. Since all of this is ultimately based on the Hebrew Bible, the arguments turned on how the text was interpreted.

As an example, let us see what was done with the verse found in Exod. 21:10. It says: "If he takes another woman, he must not deprive the first of meat, clothes and conjugal rights." That little statement about "not depriving her of her conjugal rights" leaves much to the imagination. This is how the rabbis interpreted it. The *duty* of regular intercourse, the *Onah*, was settled as follows:

1. People who do not work for a living—every day.
2. Laborers—twice a week.
3. Ass-drivers—once a week.
4. Camel-drivers—once a month.
5. Sailors—once every six months.

Even more detailed is the commentary by Rabbi Obadiah of Bertino: "Someone who was originally employed in a trade near his home and wished to change to a trade in which he would have to travel far from home, his wife may prevent him from changing, on the ground that this would make his Onah more infrequent. The exception is the scholar (whose Onah is once a week and on the sabbath); if he wished to change from being a nonworker or a laborer to a scholar, his wife may not prevent him, even though this would make his Onah more infrequent" (Mishnah, Ketuvot, 5.6).

Such is the law of Onah: the *minimum* times sexual intercourse should take place. Intercourse is regarded by the Talmud as a duty the husband owes his wife, spelled out in detail because the biblical injunction is too general.

Thus interpretation is everything, even overriding the biblical text. This is best illustrated by the following story. Mr. Shlomo sent a ten-dollar bill to a young cousin who was always asking him for money. Shlomo wrote: "Here are the ten dollars you needed so much and, by the way, there was a spelling mistake in your request. '10' is written with one zero, not two."

I repeat: interpretation is everything!

# 12

# Infallibility?

There is a wondrous story about how Buddha, because of the virtue of infallibility given to the papacy in matters of faith and morals, became a Christian saint called Josaphat.

We shall start near the end of our intriguing tale, in the year 1839. It was then that Father Huc, a French priest, set out on a mission to China. After spending a year and a half in Macao preparing himself and even learning how to disguise himself as a native, he visited Peking and Mongolia. Five years later, he took along with him Father Gobet, another French priest. Disguising themselves again, this time as lamas, and after two years of hardship and suffering, they finally penetrated the chief seats of Buddhism in Tibet.

Finally driven out by the Chinese, Huc returned to Europe in 1852. He was almost as influential in his day as Marco Polo had been five centuries earlier. He revealed such a similarity between Buddhism and his own Church that a scandal was created.

He showed that Buddhism, like Catholicism, also had its clergy in rank order, with the Grand Lama as the infallible representative of the Most High. The Grand Lama, in turn, was surrounded by minor lamas—much as the cardinals surrounded the pope. Its bishops wore miters (tall, pointed hats) and its celibate priests sported tonsures (shaven heads), wore copes (long cloaks), dressed in dalmatics (wide-sleeved garments worn by the clergy at the celebration of the Mass), and carried censures (vessels containing incense). Its vast monasteries were filled with monks and nuns vowed to poverty, chastity, and obedience. Its churches had shrines with saints and angels, images, pictures, and illuminated prayer books. Its service was very much like the Catholic Mass. The clergy sung in choirs. There was a recital of creeds, processions, mystic rites, and incense. There was the offering and adoration of the bread upon a candlelit altar. The priest drank from a chalice. Prayers were offered to the dead. The benediction was made with outstretched hands. There were fasts, confessions, and a doctrine of purgatory. All this was revealed by Father Huc.

How were these amazing, staggering facts to be accounted for? The faithful Father resorted to the old ploy. He suggested that Satan, in his anticipation of Christianity, had revealed to Buddhism this divine order. Such an explanation would have been easily accepted in the old days, but not now. The Vatican, seeing the danger by such plain revelations in the nineteenth century, put Father Huc's book on the Index, but not before it had been spread throughout the world in various translations. Father Huc was sent on no more missions.

From this came even more important discoveries, especially dealing with the claim of infallibility supposed to protect the Church against error in belief. For now literary research brought absolute evidence that the great Buddha had been canonized and enrolled among the Christian saints whose intercession was invoked, and in whose honor images, altars, and chapels were erected. All this was sanctioned by the infallible decrees of a long series of popes from the end of the sixteenth century to the end of the nineteenth. How this came about is one of the strangest errors in human history. Early in the seventh century there was composed, as is now believed, at the Convent of St. Saba near Jerusalem, a pious romance titled *Barlam and Josaphat.* The hero of the story was Josaphat, a Hindu prince converted to Christianity by Barlam.

This story, attributed to St. John of Damascus in the eighth century, became very popular and, like some who watch our modern soap operas, was soon accepted as true. As a "best seller" it was translated from the Greek original into Latin, Hebrew, Arabic, Ethiopic, and every important European language. Then it was put into the pious historical encyclopedia of Vincent of Beauvais. Most importantly of all, it became part of the *Lives of the Saints.* Thus the name of its pious hero found its way into the list of saints, where it passed without challenge until 1590, when the general subject of canonization was brought up in Rome. Pope Sixtus V, because of his infallibility, sanctioned a revised list of saints. Among those on whom he infallibly set the seal of heaven was included "The Holy Saint Josaphat of India, whose wonderful acts St. John of Damascus has related."

November 27 was the day set aside to honor the saint. The decree, enforced by successive popes for over two hundred fifty years, was again officially approved by Pious IX in 1873. One of the largest churches in Italy was dedicated to this saint, and over its main entrance was the inscription "Divo Josaphat." Inside the church was a large statue of him. Moreover, relics of this saint were found. Bones supposed to have been parts of his skeleton were presented by the Doge of Venice to a king of Portugal, only to end up as treasured relics in Antwerp.

How was this colossal error uncovered? Early in the sixteenth century, the Portuguese historian Diego Conto showed that it was identical with the legend of Buddha. Fortunately for the historian, this resemblance was again seen as a trick of Satan. As Father Huc two centuries later had rationalized, Conto claimed that

the life of Buddha was merely a diabolical counterfeit of the life of Josaphat centuries before the latter was lived and written. There the matter rested for about
three hundred years, until in 1859 Laboulaye in France, Liebrecht in Germany,
and others demonstrated that this Christian work was drawn almost word for
word from an early biography of Buddha. The only difference was that the young
Prince Buddha, instead of becoming a hermit, became a Christian, and that
instead of the name of Buddha—"Bodisat"—the more scriptural name Josaphat
was used. Not only was Buddha transformed into a Christian saint, but so was
Satan himself! But that is another bizarre tale which also points out that there can
be no such dogma as infallibility where humans are concerned.

# MIRACLES AND MAGIC

# 13

# Are There Miracles?

To be as fair as possible to the Christian position, let me set down the meaning of a miracle according to Christian theology. To them a miracle is an extraordinary event not explainable in terms of ordinary natural laws. It is an event which causes observers to assume that a divine force is behind it. These events are also evidence, or "signs," having implications much wider than the event itself. Moreover, miracles are simply not works of Providence. They are different from the types of answers gotten from prayers. Nor are they demonstrative evidence for unbelievers.

Miracles must also be distinguished from magic. In magic the wonder worker himself is supposed to possess a formula that causes the alleged result, because the alleged supernatural power is controlled by the performer. A miracle in the Christian sense depends entirely upon the divine will, and the one who works the miracle is simply an agent of God. Then, too, the miracles of God must be distinguished from satanic or demonic origin. Lastly, miracles are an absolutely essential element in Christianity: *no miracles, no Christianity.*

The first objection is to the definition of a miracle as "an extraordinary event not explainable in terms of ordinary natural laws." Since the only natural laws we do know are those provided by our sciences, any other "laws" are obviously out of our range of knowledge and therefore a mystery. To explain a mystery (miracle) with another mystery (unknown "laws"), through the agency of a third mystery (God) is to tell us nothing. To go beyond natural law is to take the path of the mystic.

There is also an inherent contradiction between the passages in the first chapter of Genesis and this element of Christian theology. Genesis tells us that God was so pleased with how he had created the world and the heavens and all the things therein that he even declared his creation to be "good." Since there is no mention in any other text that God would change his creation—or the natural

49

laws this implies—it follows that by maintaining that a miracle is not explainable in terms of natural law, Christian theology has been utterly wrong.

Under this theology Christians are now making their God fickle and self-contradictory. Because the natural laws supposedly created in Genesis are the only ones there are, for the Divine Issuer to violate his own rulings would make him completely undependable. The prophet Micah said the same thing: "For I the Lord do not change" (3:6). Furthermore, God cannot modify his own laws. If he did, he would recognize that he had been mistaken and thus would not be God. Hence he does not act by particular acts of will. There have never been, are not, and can never be any miracles.

The objection to the Christian dogma that a miracle is an "event which causes observers to assume a divine force behind it" is that science has so demythologized what used to be called "wonderful happenings" that there is little room left for the miraculous. We no longer hold that Eve's snake or Baalam's ass could talk like humans do, or that the earth is flat and has four corners, or that the rain comes from opening the windows of the heavens, or that all disease is due to demons or evil forces. The further our science progresses, the more miracles recede. Yesterday's miracles are merely the reflection of yesterday's ignorance.

It is also untrue that miracles are "different from the type of answers to prayer which do not constitute signs, or demonstrative evidence for believers." Scripture nowhere offers any apology for prayers. It simply assumes the necessity and effectiveness of man's communication with God. Admittedly, prayer is used in many ways: communion, adoration, thanksgiving, confession, and supplication. For our purposes, it is the aspect of supplication that is of interest. For, according to what is found in scripture, there are innumerable cases in which what has been asked for was granted.

We can also object to the theology that miracles can be distinguished from works of magic—just the opposite is true. Among all the ancients, Christians included, knowing the *name* of God was very important. Its knowledge gave one *magical* control over the god. This is well illustrated by Rev. 2:7: "I . . . will give him a white stone, and in the stone *a new name was written,* which no man knows save him who receives it" (italics added). This means that the new and unknown name of God is finally divulged to a few initiates. According to ancient Jewish writers, it was possible to make a "golem"—an artificial man made by supernatural means out of clay. Jewish-Christians used to believe that God had given his real hidden name to Jesus, who in turn revealed it to his believers. (See also Rev. 19:12.) Thus, contrary to Christian theology itself, there is no difference between magic and prayer.

Regarding the necessity of distinguishing the miracles of God from satanic or demonic origin (Rev. 19:20), we must confess that since Christians themselves cannot so distinguish and are often warned about being led astray by Satan (2 Cor. 11:3), then neither can the rest of us. Jesus himself, as well as Paul, shared and accepted contemporary beliefs about the existence and power of the kingdom of evil, with demonic agencies under the control of a supreme personality, Satan. In fact, one important function of Jesus was to destroy Satan, his works and his subordinates (Mark 1:24, 34; Rev. 20:10).

There is no doubt that miracles are "an absolutely essential element in Christianity." But so are they in all supernatural religions. It is because each of these belief systems rests its claim to the "only truth" upon the acceptance of its *own* miracles that no one's miracles can be accepted. Consequently, among *thinking* theists, the stratagem of "proof from miracles" is no longer even attempted.

The battle between science and religion is not between two modes of explanation. There cannot be, for religion by its dependence on miracles substitutes the unknowable for the knowable, and therefore automatically eliminates itself from what man can actually know.

# 14

# Were Miracles Important?

If you had witnessed a miracle, say, of a deformed, shrunken hand suddenly becoming whole, or of a deaf and dumb person instantly regaining his senses, or of any event defying the laws of nature or experience, wouldn't you record this act of God as most noteworthy to pass along to future readers? Of course you would. But that's just what the gospel writers did not do! All but one of the miracles in the following list were not thought significant enough by every editor to have been included in every one of the four Gospels!

See for yourself . . .

JESUS' MIRACLES

*Healing*

> The nobleman's son: John 4
> The lame man: John 5
> Peter's mother-in-law: Matthew 8, Mark 1, Luke 4
> The synagogue demoniac: Mark 1
> The leper: Matthew 8, Mark 1, Luke 5
> The paralytic: Matthew 9, Mark 2, Luke 5
> The withered hand: Matthew 12, Mark 3, Luke 6
> The centurion's servant: Matthew 8, Mark 7
> The blind and dumb demoniac: Matthew 12, Luke 11
> The woman with the issue of blood: Matthew 9, Mark 5, Luke 8
> The demoniac: Mark 5, Luke 8
> The two demoniacs: Matthew 8
> The blind man: Mark 10, Luke 18
> The two blind men: Matthew 20

The demon-possessed girl: Matthew 15, Mark 7
The synagogue demoniac: Mark 1

*Raising from the dead*

The widow's son: Luke 7
Jairus's daughter: Matthew 9, Mark 5, Luke 8
Lazarus: Luke 11

*Feeding multitudes*

The 4,000: Matthew 15, Mark 8

*Signs*

Turning water into wine: John 2
Catch of fish: Luke 5
Stilling the storm: Matthew 8, Mark 4, Luke 8
Walking on water: Matthew 14, Mark 6

Some of the miracles described in the oldest Gospel according to Mark were not even good enough for the other disciples. They had to heighten them for a greater affect! Take, for example, the miracle as described in Mark in which Jesus cures just one man possessed by demons by driving them into a herd of swine which then drowned. Matthew jazzes this up by adding one more demoniac to his Gospel, so that Jesus now cures two persons! Or compare the miracle of the cure of the blind man in Mark with Matthew's treatment. Here we find not one but two blind men healed! If Matthew had to take the stand in a civil court of law, he would have been punished for perjury.

There's more. The *coup de grâce* is what might be called the "miracle genealogist." As the Bible evolved, the later miracles echoed the earlier ones. After all, the later prophets certainly had to be able to produce the same miracles as their predecessors—or even top their act. Jesus' miracles of healing and reviving mirror those of Elijah and Elisha. Actually, some of Jesus' supposed wonders can be traced as far back as Moses. For example, Jesus' walk on the Sea of Galilee owes its ancestry to Elijah and Elisha's passage of the Jordon. This, in turn, reflects Moses' crossing of the Red ("reed") Sea. Also, feeding of the multitudes is of the same legendary source as the story of Elijah's increasing the widow's flour.

Now I ask you: if some of these miracles had to be retouched in bolder colors for apologetic reasons, if some were merely retreads of older wonders found in the Old Testament, and if all these prodigies were not considered to have been bonafide enough to have been repeated in each of the four Gospels, then in the name of rationality, are we not entitled to question their validity and importance?

# 15

# The Magic Is the Same—
# Only the Techniques Have Changed

An ancient Greek worshiping at his temple was astonished and enraptured to witness, at the instant the sacrificial flame of the altar was lit, the statue of Bacchus suddenly pour wine, the idol of Diana stream forth milk, and the Serpent applauding their action by hissing, all of which were accompanied by the noise of drums and cymbals. He believed that all this was due to divine intervention. If you were that worshiper, wouldn't you?

We know that Bacchus was considered the discoverer of the vine and wine, Diana of milk, and the Serpent the first cause of all things. Since sacrifices had to be made to the gods in order to obtain benefits like wine and milk, their actual materialization in front of the worshiper's eyes demonstrated the existence of the gods. What the mass of ancient worshipers did not know, but which we moderns do, is that these miraculous demonstrations were merely tricks employed by the priests, much as stage magicians perform today. How were they done?

Our main source of information is Heron of Alexandria, a Greek geometer and mechanician of the third century after Christ. Contrary to our biased views that the Greeks, because they were so dependent on slave labor, utterly failed to develop the mechanical arts, we learn from Heron's treatise that the Greeks were quite advanced. He describes wheels turned by ropes on shafts or axles, or moved by ropes attached to weights. He tells of liquids moved through pipes by siphons and suction activated by the heat of combustibles or of the sun through a concentrating lens. Heron reports wheels with teeth (what we now call gears) for accurate movements and measurement, plus a host of other mechanical devices that were the forerunners of similar, though improved, later "inventions" of mechanical contrivances.

Heron described how this mechanical know-how was applied to one of the temple's magical devices called "The Triumph of Bacchus." The unit consisted of a moveable case called a "theater." At its upper part there was a platform.

54

From this arose a cylindrical temple whose six columns supported a roof. On top of the roof was the figure of Victory with spread wings and holding a crown in her right hand. Standing in the center of the temple was Bacchus, whose left hand held a thyrsus (a staff tipped with a pine cone and entwined with vine leaves). His right hand gripped a cup. At his feet lay a panther. In front and behind the god were two altars of combustible materials. Close to the six columns were Bacchantes—figures representing priestesses or women votaries of the god. They were placed in any position fancied by the temple priest.

After the worshipers had assembled, said Heron, the *automatic apparatus* was set in motion—the theater appeared to move itself! After stopping at a selected spot, the theater's altar in front of Bacchus lit up and, at the same time, milk and water spurted from his thyrsus and cup. This was followed by another round of the Bacchantes to the sound of drums and cymbals. After the "dance" was finished, the moveable theater was returned to its original position. Thus ended the spectacular sight of the glorification of the god Bacchus.

How does Heron explain how "The Triumph of Bacchus" worked? The theater moved on three wheels concealed in the base. This may have been the first known description of a "locomotive" or moving vehicle. Heron even described how the wheels were arranged and proportioned so that the theater could move in a circle.

Heron divulged much more. The combustible materials were placed on a metal altar in whose interior were hidden small lit-up lamps separated from the combustibles by a metal plate. The plate was drawn aside at the proper time by a small chain and, presto, the sacrificial fire flamed up!

The wine, water, and milk came from a double reservoir hidden under the roof of the temple and were connected by tubes through the arms and hands of the god to holes in the thyrsus and cup. A key, maneuvered by cords, alternately opened and closed the holes through which the liquid poured. The noise of the drum and cymbals, said Heron, came from falling granules of lead contained in a hidden box with an automatic sliding valve. For the drum noises the granules fell on an inclined tambourine, after which they rebounded against little cymbals in the interior of the theater's base. By properly winding cords around vertical bobbins instead of on horizontal axles, the half turns of Victory and Bacchus as well as the full revolutions of the Bacchantes were achieved.

There were many other mechanical contrivances for producing the illusions to which the ancient religions owed their power: trumpet sounders, temple door openers, altar fire extinguishers, dicaimeters (vessels which allowed only a definite amount of liquid to escape), miraculous containers (like coffins), drinking horns, magical pitchers and bottles, hydraulic organs, whirling eolophiles (precursor to the steam engine), "perpetual" burning lamps, and odometers (for measuring distances on the ground).

Modern clerics no longer have to resort to the material and mechanical stage magic promoted by ancient temple priests. Instead, it is now all done by spiritualizing the material basis, like transforming the wine and wafer of the Catholic

Mass into the blood and body of Christ. The magic is the same—only the techniques have changed!

# RELIGION AND MENTAL ILLNESS

# 16

# Religion Is Injurious to Your Mental Health

Some time ago statistics on the religious make-up of prisoners in Pennsylvania were 65 percent Catholics, 26 percent Protestant, 6 percent Jewish, 2 percent "pagans," and 1 percent irreligious. These could have been matched across the country. Like a neon sign they flashed the message that religious instruction does not improve morality. We atheists have been saying this for so long that we have laryngitis. James Leuba, a famous religious investigator, put it this way: "Instead of being the allies of the philosophical attitude, the religions have been and remain its strongest opponents."

A morality based on religion is like a cap pistol used for shooting foxes molesting chickens—you only succeed in frightening the chickens even more. Instead of evoking a satisfactory response to the real world, faith in the "Good Shepherd" merely keeps you in the world of illusion. Clearly, one negative result of the religious conditioning of the child may be his emotional malnutrition, making him a psychological pygmy for the rest of his life.

One psychological technique devastatingly wielded by religion is its "guilt complex." If it isn't "original sin" or subsequent "sin," it's the "sin of omission" where a magical ritual has not been performed or an incantation was not mouthed properly. If not these, then you can conclude that God is "testing" someone.

"Be ye perfect as your Father in heaven is perfect" (Matt. 5:48) leads one to try to step so high that he must do a Buster Keaton emotional pratfall. Such a command must foster massive feelings of guilt because no one can be as perfect as God is supposed to be.

If this isn't enough to make you wear a "hair shirt," then there's the concept of going hell to keep you in line. If you're not afraid of hell, Calvin's description of sinners in the kingdom of the Devil should do it: "Forever harassed with a dreadful tempest, they shall feel themselves torn asunder by an angry God and transfixed and penetrated by mortal stings, terrified by the thunderbolts of God

59

and broken by the weight of his hand, so that to sink into any gulf would be more tolerable than to stand for a moment in these terrors. Even infants bring their damnation with them."

Can you remember, or imagine, this hot poker on your emotional hide as a preacher continues the harangue week after week? Some of our political leaders have been so traumatized that they believe the biblically predicted battle of Armageddon will be fought in our lifetime!

Prejudice is one of the natural diseases of the religiously twisted. Gordon Allport stings us back to reality: "On the average, churchgoers and professedly religious people have considerably more prejudice than do nonchurchgoers and nonbelievers. Brotherhood and bigotry are intertwined in all religion."[1]

If you belong to an in-group that believes it is the only one who has a handle on the truth, then ipso facto, all others are to be treated as inferiors, defectives, or deadly enemies to be wiped out. The outsider to a Jew is a "goy," to the Christian a "heretic," and to the Muslim an "idolator."

Alexander Feinsilver says this, too: "It is not in human nature to hold that the most precious thing conceivable depends upon the possession of a particular faith, and yet to tolerate those who condemn that faith."[2]

Lastly, there's that devastating "iron curtain" that's drawn across the mind, preventing analysis of the irrationality of religion. To prevent this religions have set up their own schools, and today there is a clamor for a voucher system to enable those schools to accommodate even more children.

It is too bad that the fruits of rationality, our scientific and technical know-how, may be used for either good or evil, allowing the inculcation of superstition. The personal computer and desktop printing are indifferent as to whether the Bible or the theory of relativity is printed. As the famous poet and atheist Percy Bysshe Shelley so aptly remarked: "The crime of inquiry is one which religion has never forgiven." To quote a more contemporary spokesman, Professor H. N. Wieman of the School of Divinity at the University of Chicago: "Religion has blinded men to facts, magnified delusions, and hindered men from making adaptations to things as they are."

The prescription needed to teach children to respond rationally is to sever the religious umbilical cord as soon as possible and to teach in such a way as to promote analysis and evaluation so as to base judgments on evidence. If we do not do this, if children are placed for indoctrination in religious schools and institutions, then don't be surprised to discover that religion was injurious to their health.

## NOTES

1. Gordon Allport, *Personality and Social Encounter* (Boston: Beacon Press, 1960).

2. Alexander Feinsilver (ed.), *The Talmud Today* (New York: St. Martin's Press, 1980).

# 17

# The Theological Roots
# of Arab Anti-Semitism

Since World War II Christianity has been rightly taken over the coals for its centuries of anti-Semitism which was a major contributing factor that led to that horror called the Holocaust. What is not known and even less publicized, however, is that this virus also permeates the Arab world. Just as the New Testament is laced with anti-Semitism, so is the holy book of Islam, the Koran.

During the expansion of Islam most of the conquered territory was Christian. This made it necessary to allow Christians to continue to use their Greek language as well as to practice their religion and read their Bibles. Thus the anti-Semitism of Christians was added to that already accepted by the Muslims.

The celebrated controversialist al-Jahaz (850 C.E.) cited in an anti-Christian polemic four reasons why the faithful (that is, the Muslims) held a better opinion of the Christians than of the Jews: Christians wielded power in Byzantium and elsewhere, whereas the Jews were completely powerless; Christians engaged in the secular sciences whereas the Jews did not; Christians assimilated and took Muslim names more readily than the Jews did; and Christians engaged in more respectable occupations than the Jews did.

In the same period, the historian al-Tabari observed that Christians "bear witness against the Jews morning and night." Thus, a number of anti-Semitic traditions and legends from Christian folklore were adopted and absorbed into Islam.

The language and purpose of the Koran is even more harsh in its treatment of the Jews than is the New Testament. In Mohammed's teachings, the Jews are cast aside by Allah because of their disobedience. Here are some prooftexts from their holy book:

"They [the Jews] say, 'Our hearts are the wrappings which preserve God's word: we need no more.' Nay, God's curse is on them for blasphemy: little is it they believe" (2:88). This means that the Jews in their arrogance claimed all

61

wisdom and knowledge were enclosed within their own hearts. This claim was not only arrogant but blasphemous.

"Of the Jews there are those who displaced words from their right places, and say, 'We hear and we obey;' . . . with a twist of their tongues and a slander to the Faith [Islam]. . . . When they said aloud 'We hear and obey,' they then whispered 'We disobey' " (4:46).

"They are men whom God has cursed: And these whom God hath cursed, thou will find, have no one to help" (4:52).

"But because of their breach of their Covenant, We cursed them, and made their hearts grow hard" (5:14). This means that because the Jews breached their Covenant, God withdrew his grace from them.

"Say, O People of the Book [the Jews]! Do ye disapprove of us for no other reason than we believe in God, and the revelation that hath come to us . . . that most of you are rebellious and disobedient?" (5:62). This means that the Jews hate them because the Muslims believe in God and the Jewish scriptures. Jews hate us because we obey and you are in rebellion against God. Did you not incur the curse of God? (See Deut. 11:28, 28:15–68, Hosea 8:14, 9:1.) The Jews forsook God and worshiped evil (Jer. 16:11–13).

"And had it not been that God had decreed banishment for them, He would certainly have punished them in this world; and in the hereafter they shall certainly have the punishment of the Fire" (59:3). This means that the Jews will burn in hellfire.

"Those who reject our signs, we shall soon cast into the fire. As often as their skins are roasted through, we shall change them for fresh skins, that they may taste the penalty: for God is exalted in power" (4:56). This is a better description of hell than any found in the New Testament.

"Ye are the best of peoples, evolved for mankind, enjoining what is right, forbidding what is wrong, and believing in God. If only the People of the Book had faith, it were best for them: among them are some who have faith, but most of them are perverted transgressors" (3:110). This means that Muslims are the best people on earth, and if the Jews and Christians had also believed in Mohammed and the Koran, things would have gone a lot better for them.

"Mohammed is not the father of any of your men, but he is the Apostle of God, and the Seal of the Prophets" (33:40). This means that Mohammed proclaimed himself the last and culminating prophet—or the Seal of the Prophets (see Deut. 18:18). When a document is sealed, it is complete, and there can be no more additions. Thus there will be no prophet after Mohammed.

Mohammed connected himself with the People of the Book through the following rationale. Isaac was Abraham's son and Jacob his grandson. His other children included Ishmael. Each became a fountainhead of prophecy and revelation—Isaac and Jacob through Moses, and Ishmael through the holy Apostle Mohammed.

It is interesting how the modern Sunni also rejects the Jews. The Sunni are one of the two great Muslim sects.

"Judaism is not a monolithic religion but a tribal creed. . . . The 'God of Israel' . . . is obsessed with his people. . . . He watches their daily obscenities and their sins without moving a hair. After a few pretentious overtures in the first pages of Genesis, He has spent all his time, energy and intelligence, while the rest of the cosmos rotted, to dispossess a wretched little people of their land, put them to the sword and enter 'his people' into possession of the land and whatever tree, beast or child who escaped his 'wrath.' The truth is that this god never traveled, has never seen the world, not to speak of making it. He is a 'country' man whose world ended with his tribe, beyond which everything and everybody is equally foreign and equally an enemy. In short, he is a regional, tribal, separatist god, with whom monotheism has absolutely nothing to do."

No further commentary is necessary. Islam mirrors the same anti-Semitism found in Christianity. Just as we can trace the response to the Jews back to its source in the New Testament, so we have seen that fertile ground for the theological roots of anti-Semitism also lies in the holy Koran of Mohammed.

# 18

# Believe It or Not!

The hen that lays the biggest egg usually does the least cackling. Religion is no exception. What has been done in its name has laid plenty of eggs, eggs which are certainly not worth cackling about. Below is a short list of such banalities that it is a wonder that any rational person would support a religion. As you read and think about them, try not to groan or guffaw so as to disturb anyone.

1. In London during the 1700s, you could buy an insurance policy to protect you from going to hell. (Sounds like the insurance policies those who belonged to Heaven's Gate bought.)

2. The famous feminist and writer, Dorothy Parker, called her parrot Onan, because it was always spilling its seed on the ground!

3. In the courts of the Roman Empire, instead of swearing oaths on the Bible, men swore to the truth of their statements while holding their balls. Hence the word "testify," from "testicles."

4. In 1456, Pope Calixtus III declared Halley's comet an agent of the devil—and excommunicated it!

5. Saint Boniface is the patron saint of sodomy.

6. In the fourteenth century the Church opposed the idea of insurance because insurance defied financial disasters sent by God.

7. Rather than throwing them out of the Church, Henry I found a new punishment for priests who forgot their vows and had sex. He created a new tax they had to pay.

8. India may have been the birthplace of Buddhism, yet only 1 percent of its population are practicing Buddhists.

9. Theologians in the Middle Ages, having decided that the Virgin Mary must have been impregnated through the ear, declared that all women should keep their ears covered since they functioned as genitals.

10. The Japanese emperor had always been regarded as a living god, so no

one was allowed to touch him. Even his tailor had to estimate his godlike inside leg measurement from across the room.

11. The Vatican has a storeroom full of carved genitals. They were removed from statues and replaced by fig leaves when the Roman Catholic Church decided the sight of them would lead to impure thoughts.

12. Not every country will celebrate the millennium. January 1, 2000, will be 5760 in the Jewish calendar, 1420 in the Islamic calendar, and 1921 in the Hindu calendar.

13. Bishop Isidor of Seville (560–636) was the first Christian to condemn transvestism. He chewed out New Year dancers in Spain: "These miserable creatures transform themselves into monsters, womanizing their masculine faces and making female gestures, romping, stamping, clapping, both sexes together in a ring dance, a shameful thing, a host with dulled senses intoxicated by wine!"

14. The Roman Catholic Church tried its best to cut down on *licit* sex. First, coitus was made illegal on Sundays, Wednesdays, and Fridays—which effectively removed the equivalent of five months of the year. Then it was banned for forty days before Easter and for forty days before Christmas and for three days before communion (and there were rules requiring frequent attendance at communion). It was also made illegal from the time of conception to forty days after parturition. Finally, it was forbidden during any penance.

Enough, already! With these you can win a few bar bets, impress your friends with your esoteric knowledge, and maybe, just maybe, convince someone else to discard their religious irrationalities.

# ARCHEOLOGY
# AND THE BIBLE

# 19

# The Spade Is Mightier Than the Word:
## Part 1

R ight now, I'm popped off—like the safety valve of a pressure cooker—and my disposition is like an untipped waiter's. I'm fed up with reading the conclusions of some of the leading archeologists and their popularizers who lie like secondhand car salesmen.

One of their top scholars, archeologist Nelson Glueck, says in his essay "The Bible and Archeology" that "the truths of the Bible expressed in preachment and prediction, in legend and law, in history and myth . . . are not susceptible to proof of any kind. They can neither be buttressed nor invalidated archeologically. New discovery . . . can never replace or refute or corroborate its religious values. The finds of archeological exploration . . . in no wise affect its religious propositions or ethical decrees."

This is one of the finest red herrings I have ever come across that preserves the "infallibility and inspiration" of biblical theology. Ever since the history and science of the Bible have chucked away much of the Bible as mostly old wives' tales, there has been a super effort to save its theology from a similar fate.

Yet, Glueck doesn't hesitate to destroy one popularizer's efforts. Here is what he states about Werner Keller's best-selling *The Bible As History*: "Sparkingly written and easy to read, it is a book full of interesting information and almost equally interesting misinformation. . . . The basic purpose of his book, which almost completely nullifies its many excellencies, is to characterize the Bible as a chronicle of true history . . . it simply cannot be emphasized enough that the Bible was not compiled for a strictly historical purpose."

Thus Glueck turns Keller from a Superman of biblical authority into a Minnie Mouse of biblical fables!

Keller, on the other hand, sides with Glueck in that both emphasize a hands-off policy toward the theology of the Bible. This is how Keller puts it: "Thanks to the findings of the archeologists, many of the biblical narratives can be understood better now than ever before. There are, of course, theological insights which can only be dealt with in terms of the Word of God."

There we have it, from both a professional archeologist and a best-selling popularizer: archeology can neither prove nor disprove the theology of the Bible. This is enough hot air to lift the Goodyear blimp far off the ground!

They avoid telling us what we want to know: does archeology really have nothing to say about the theology of the Bible? The answer is that archeology certainly does shed light on biblical theology!

Following are refutations to three very important theological myths: the myth that the Jerusalem Temple was the exclusive and only place where sacrifices could be made to God; the myth that the biblical injunctions against the practice of magic were carried out to the letter by the Jews; and the myth that the Jews faithfully followed the commandment of the Decalogue not to make a graven or plastic image of God. And all this will be done by using the evidence unearthed by the archeologist's spade!

This first essay on archeology will deal only with the myth of the exclusiveness of the Jerusalem Temple. That the sacrificial cult and its priests were "endowed with a special sanctity" goes back to the time when it was established by Solomon. But its *exclusive* position as the *only* place for the sacrificial cult is usually tied in with the reforms of King Josiah, about 621 B.C.E. From the book of Kings we learn that a systematic attempt was made to do away with all cult centers outside of Jerusalem, thereby forcing all sacrifices to the Jerusalem Temple.

From then on, the central position of the Jerusalem Temple supposedly became part of the religious system of Judaism. Its rebuilding was due to those Jews who had returned from the Babylonian captivity. Rabbinic sources are unanimous in that the Jerusalem Temple was the only permissible cult center of the Jews.

For the Jews of the Diaspora, the Temple also played a very special role. During the Second Temple period there were a series of disasters, forcing the Jews to scatter all over the known word—hence the word "Diaspora," or dispersal. In the eighth century, Assyria grabbed up many of the ten tribes of the Northern kingdom of Israel. Then during the early sixth century there were repeated deportations to Mesopotamia. At the same time we hear of Jews in Egypt who were defying the prophet Jeremiah, preferring to worship the "Queen of Heaven" instead of Yahweh. In the fifth century, there were Jewish mercenary soldiers in Upper Egypt. From then on, the number of Jews living outside the Holy Land grew considerably. During the final pre-Christian centuries, the Jerusalem Temple became so important that every Jew in the Diaspora paid "his Peter's Pence" or temple tax.

Yet, and this is the crucial information, from the sixth century on we hear of a series of Jewish temples outside Jerusalem! Excavations have uncovered a temple at Arad, near Beth-Sheva, which not only survived the reforms of king Josiah but was patterned exactly on the Jerusalem sanctuary!

One century later, in the fifth, the Jews of Elephantine built a temple in their colony located in Upper Egypt. We know this because a number of papyrus letters and documents from the colony have been unearthed. For our purposes the importance of these documents is that the temple at Elephantine was maintained in spite of the theological injunction against any temples being outside of Jerusalem. These letters tell us that because their own temple had burned down they had to send for help to the governors of Judah and Samaria.

This is quite an eye-opener, for it tells us first, that the Jews of Elephantine felt their temple quite unexceptional and legitimate; and second, that in the Holy Land itself there were two competing temples, one in Jerusalem, the other in Shechem, the capital of Samaria.

Another temple was dug up in Transjordan, at a site called Araq el-Emir, dating back to the second century B.C.E. This temple was started by a certain Hyrcanus who was a member of the Tobiad family which, in turn, intermarried with the family of the high priestly family in Jerusalem. This means that there was absolutely no excuse on the part of Hyrcanus to be ignorant of the injunction forbidding the erection of a competing temple.

Our next proof concerns a temple builder who was the son of Onias III, the last of the Zadokite High Priests. He was deposed by Antiochus IV Epiphanes in 175-174 B.C.E., fleeing to Egypt. With the permission of the Egyptian ruler, Onias IV built a temple and founded a military colony at a place called Leontopolis, near Alexandria. Here we have the incredible act of the son of the Zadokite High Priest of the Jerusalem Temple actually building his own despite the long-standing biblical prohibition against it!

The Jewish general and priest Josephus wrote about this as though there were nothing strange about building a new temple. He also wrote about the Dead Sea sect of Jews which, according to archeologists, also made animal sacrifices at their headquarters in Qumran, since this sect rejected the Jerusalem Temple.

Thus, from the sixth century onward, there existed a number of Jewish temples inside and outside of Israel—all of them apart from the Jerusalem Temple. There can be no doubt that the biblical sources as well as a number of leading archeologists and popularizers have lied to us.

Can anyone doubt that the exclusive status of the Jerusalem Temple was but another theological myth now properly buried by the archeologist's spade, a spade that has proven mightier than the word of the Bible?

The next chapter will demonstrate that the biblical theology that forbids the use of magic by Jews was also a myth.

# 20

# The Spade Is Mightier Than the Word:
# Part 2

Although there are theological statements in the Bible prohibiting all forms of magic, many Jews and Christians ignored them. The Bible itself is its own best witness to their continuation despite the Bible's injunction.

The Bible gives a good laundry list of magical don'ts in Deut. 18:10–12: "There must be none among you who makes his son or daughter pass through fire, no augur or soothsayer or diviner or sorcerer, no one who casts spells or traffics with ghosts and spirits, no medium or magician, and no necromancer. Those who do such things are abominable to the Lord."

That this was a colossal pious lie is well illustrated when King Saul himself actually defies these prohibitions and seeks guidance from the Witch of Endor (1 Sam. 28)! Even the Talmud sanctions magic, provided it's the benevolent kind, coming only from God. A whole episode of sorcery is referred to—and permitted to boot!—in a feat ascribed to Rabbis Hanina and Oshaiah in which they create a three-year-old calf every sabbath eve through study and the application of the mystical *Book of Creation*!

Archeologists come into the picture by describing an important area of magic which they have unearthed, that of amulets. They were worn around the neck, wrist, arm, or ankle as a protection against injury, sickness, and evil, and to bring good luck. Talismans had the same function and were usually rings or stones with engraved figures or symbols.

The esoteric "knowledge" for which these amulets stood had been accumulated over thousand years by the civilizations of the Mediterranean and the Persian Gulf, shared equally by Assyrians, Phoenicians, Jews, Egyptians, and many others.

One of these amulets was called the Saharon, usually made of gold, and represented the moon in its third quarter. The amulet was worn in the center of the forehead attached to a headband or ribbon, with the two points of the crescent moon facing upward. Such were the designs of the amulet of the moon god shown on Sumerian Saharons, and of Ishtar, the moon goddess of the later Babylonians.

The Saharon was replaced by the Totaphoth, a headband with an amulet attached. At first its amulets were inscribed stones; later, texts written on parchment were substituted.

Parchment with verses of the Old Testament were also placed in a slim container of wood or metal called a "Mezuzah." Today's Jews still attach it to their doorways. A special amulet of this kind used to be secured to an expectant mother's room to ensure a safe childbirth.

Then there are those amulets in the form of seals for stamping letters and documents because their magical powers was thought to protect these communications. Such was the origin of the Star or Shield of David which is formed by two inverted triangles superimposed on one another and which is now a universally recognized Jewish symbol. The earliest known example dug up appears on a scaraboid agate seal from the Palestine of the seventh century B.C.E. It occurs there with the name of its owner and represents a magical sign of power.

This six-pointed star was also found in association with a portrait of the goddess Astarte on a plaque discovered at the biblical site of Libnah. It also figures on several Mesopotamian seals. In the Greco-Roman period it often adorns the early synagogues of Galilee.

Why did it become a symbol of magic? In Hebrew one of the triangles making up the six-pointed star was called "esh" while the other was called "mayim." It was imaginatively thought that together they spelled "shamayim" ("heaven"), a recognized euphemism for God. When used in magic this hexagram became a written substitute for the Ineffable Name, just as "Adonai" ("Lord") was a verbal one. Even in Christian magical writings, each of the four outer triangles is usually labeled with one of the Hebrew letters of the Tetragrammaton "YHWH" ("Yahweh"). It should also be noted that in alchemy these triangles represented the four cardinal points, and therefore convey the notion of the universality and omnipresence of God.

A number of amulets show Jewish heroes like Daniel with the lions, the sacrifice of Isaac, Jonah, as well as emblems of the menorah and Jewish words and names.

At a later time, pagan-Jewish themes are found. One has "the Cavalier God who spears evil as a woman or a lion at his feet, and is specifically named Solomon, the master magician of them all." This design must have been quite popular, for it survived more than the others. It was taken over by Christians who dropped the word Solomon and made the spear into a long cross.

It should be clear, then, that the Jews embraced magic from all sources, putting on their graves and synagogues lions, eagles, winged Victories, Torah scrolls, Helios, wreaths, fishes, ethrog* and lulav†, and pagan deities like

---

*An ethrog is a fruit, a sort of citron.

†A lulav is a staff consisting of intertwined boughs of palm, willow, and myrtle. Such a staff, tipped with pine cone and twined with ivy, was carried by Dionysian revelers—further proof that the Jews, like all their neighbors, have assimilated pagan customs.

Aphrodite and Isis. Like their pagan contemporaries, the Jews also wanted to protect themselves against all the evils of life and to secure all of its bounties.

In 2 Macc. 12:32–45, there is a most instructive story. It tells how Judas Maccabee, in examining his own dead soldiers, found that each was wearing "an amulet of the idols of Jamnia!"

Another informative area deals with magic formulas. A large number of jars dating from the first century bear Hebrew and Syrian inscriptions of long lists of names of demons and spirits. Jewish names for God flood these magic formulas. Pagan necromancers (those who called up and communicated with the spirits of the dead) used the Jewish names of God in their incantations and exorcisms. Many Jewish prisoners in Rome, especially women, earned their living by practicing magic.

Even though spokesmen for Christianity deny it is a religion of magic, it can easily be shown to be otherwise. Two examples will be enough to prove this.

The report of the baptism of Jesus in Mark 1:11 goes like this: "It happened . . . that Jesus . . . was baptized in the Jordon by John. At the moment when he came out of the water, he saw the heavens torn open and the Spirit, like a dove, descended upon him. And a voice spoke from heaven: 'Thou art my Son, my Beloved; on thee my favor rests.' "

Where did this myth come from? Why, from the magical papyri! In the book *The Demotic Magical Papyrus of London and Leiden,* we read of a man who made a god by a rite of purification followed by the opening of the heavens and the coming of a spirit. Similar myths can be found in other magical papyri.

The second example concerns itself with the Coptic church of Egypt, one of the first of the Christian churches, and its belief in the magic of amulets. The ancient Egyptian ankh (symbol for life) also was adopted as a Christian symbol. On a very old Coptic amulet now in the famous British Museum, the Virgin Mary is shown seated under a tree, holding in one hand an ankh and in the other an orthodox Christian cross.

There is no further need to explore in depth the magical terrain of the New Testament with its world dominated by the supernatural personalities of Beelzebub, Satan/Serpent, and the Prince of the Air the Devil, all the lessor demons, the Holy Ghost and the Paraclete, the miracles performed by exorcisms, the belief in the magical name of Jesus, the taking up of serpents, the drinking of poison—it's all there!

Even though the Bible and its archeological apologists insist that the Jews and Christians were uncompromisingly hostile to magic, their own evidence proves otherwise. In view of the penalty of death for those who engaged in magic as described in Exod. 22:18, it's a wonder that the pages of the Bible aren't strewn with the dead bodies of its practitioners!

The next chapter will demonstrate that the injunction against making any image of God is also a bald-faced lie—and should be properly buried by the archeologist's spade.

# 21

# The Spade Is Mightier Than the Word: Part 3

Here's what Gershon Scholem, a world-famous Jewish scholar, says in his article "Anthropomorphism" in the latest edition of the prestigious *Encyclopedia Judaica*: "There is no evidence of any physical representation of God in Jewish history (in contradistinction to the worship of Canaanite and other foreign gods by Israelites). . . . Biblical Hebrew is the only fully developed language which has no specific term for the notion of 'goddess.' "

Who's he kidding? Scholem should have read page 318 of the same volume his article was in. There he would have seen a quarter-page size of the goddess Astarte, dated about the tenth century B.C.E., from in Tel Zeror, this being only one of many found in the Israelite strata! It's true that there was no word for "goddess," but there were more than enough names used for the female deity: Astarte, Anath, and Ashtoreth!

These goddesses are explained in the same volume. What the Jews did was to deliberately corrupt the name "strt" ("astart" or "asteret") to conform with the vocalization of the Hebrew word "boshet" ("shame"). There's no question that Astarte (or Boshet) was a fierce warrior goddess as well as the goddess of love and fertility. What does Scholem think the Old Testaments prophets were raising Cain about, if not, among other practices, the worship of the goddess?

But this is only one person's pious lie. Our main concern is with the myth which Scholem and others try to perpetuate—that there has never been any physical representation of God in Jewish history.

Although Jews have interlaced their Bible with anthropomorphic concepts of God, his representation in any plastic form is clearly forbidden by Mosaic Law. It is well known by anyone who has read the Old Testament that God has been given human attributes like eyes, hand, a tongue, speech, feet, a head, and even a backside. What is not realized is that he has been represented in Jewish art all the way up to the eighteenth century!

75

In the frescoes of the synagogue at Dura-Europus (300 C.E.), there can be seen the hand of God stretching forth from heaven. In certain cases where they depict the visions of Ezekiel, these representations might be justified as an illustration of the biblical text 37:1 where the prophet said: "the hand of the Lord was upon me."

No such excuse, however, can be used to explain the fact that at Dura-Europus, and at Bet Alfa too, there are representations of the Divine Hand extending from heaven to prevent Abraham from sacrificing his son. That this was deliberate is proven from the fact that the biblical passage says that the patriarch was restrained, not by God's hand, but by the voice of an angel!

This plastic tradition was continued in medieval Jewish illustrated manuscripts. In the Sarajevo Haggada there is the figure of a man in repose that illustrates God taking his rest after his acts of creation. Later, this theme was taken up in documents and in printed books. One of the scenes published in Augsburg in 1540 shows God engaged in the work of creation and in the creation of Eve.

God was also depicted in scenes from the vision of Ezekiel on the engraved title page of a manuscript (1742); on the engraved border of an Italian manuscript (1700); and in a representation of the Vision of Jacob at Bethel on the title page of a manuscript from Frankfort (1698).

Then there is the depiction in stone relief of God appearing to the infant Samuel, based on 1 Sam. 3:10, on the gravestone of a Sephardic Jew in Amsterdam (1717). This is especially remarkable in view of the biblical prohibition of graven images.

As you have seen, three very important theological dogmas have been shown by the archeologist's spade to be pious lies: the exclusiveness of the Jerusalem Temple, the nonpractice of magic, and the nonrepresentation of images of God. Fortunately for us laymen the spade has now proven to be mightier than the Word.

# 22

# Plagiarism or Research?

**D**id the biblical authors borrow or steal a good deal of their material from others? Archeological and historical investigations have shown that far too much of what goes for authentic biblical history and theology was taken from Israel's neighbors.

It was during their sojourn in Egypt that the Hebrews adopted a clerical organization which was unknown to their desert ancestors.

Their adoption of the cult of angels came from the "cherubim" of Mesopotamia and the celestial beings of Persian tradition.

The story of Genesis and of the Flood was one of the outstanding features of the whole Mesopotamian tradition.

The code of Hammurabi, which can be seen in the Louvre, a handsome black stone on which this Babylonia king of the beginning of the second millennium engraved his laws, contains ordinances similar to those of Moses.

The Mosaic laws also resemble the commandments to be read in the Book of the Dead from Egypt.

The Song of Songs is related to some wedding hymns found on the banks of the Nile.

The compiler of the section of the book of Proverbs often called "Sayings of the Wise Men" was influenced by the Egyptian sage Amenemope.

Psalm 104 was modeled on a hymn composed in honor of Pharaoh Akhenaton's sun god.

The Greek book of Wisdom used the vocabulary of the Alexandrian philosophers, and to some extent their philosophy. Such resemblances can also be discovered in the Gospels of the New Testament. For instance, the author of Luke apparently studied a book on medicine written by Dioscurides, a Greek who served as doctor in the Roman army.

Taking material from one person is called stealing. Taking from two or more is called research. Speaking plainly, the ancient Jews stole a good deal of their legends, myths, wisdom, history, and theology from others far more advanced. They should acknowledge their indebtedness instead of palming off their writings as divinely revealed.

# JESUS:
# WARTS AND ALL

# 23

# The Devolution of Divine Revelation

"Revelation" is the doctrine of God's making himself and his relevant truths known to man. "Progressive revelation" means that God's revelations have been presented on a higher, more sophisticated and perfect plane as time has unfolded. Thus Christians believe that their religious revelations are the finest in the long train of God's truths which began during the barbarity of the Hebrew tribes, finally culminating in the high moral standards of Jesus Christ. In other words, the revelation of God achieves its consummation in Jesus Christ, in whom all that was scattered and fragmented in the Jewish dispensation is gathered into a unity and fulness (Heb. 1:1–2). This thesis was an attempt by Christians embarrassed by the low state of morals in the Old Testament to apply the theory of evolution to biblical morality. Is this theme correct? Can we discover areas where revelation has actually regressed?

In the first dispensation, that of the Jews, God reveals to men one of his great commandments: "Be fruitful and multiply; and fill the earth and subdue it; and have dominion over . . . every living thing that moves upon the earth" (Gen. 1:28). Contrast this necessary injunction with the one revealed by Jesus Christ: "For there have been eunuchs who have been so from birth, and there are eunuchs who have been made eunuchs by men, and there are eunuchs who have made themselves eunuchs for the sake of the kingdom of heaven. He who is able to receive this, let him receive it" (Matt. 19:10–12). Now ask yourself this: which revelation is more barbarous? Who but a man suffering from an aberration would even consider, let alone recommend, such an uncivilized and unnatural deed?

The second part of this revelation is also denied: "to subdue the earth:" For 1 John 2:15–16 gives us a new revelation: "[but we must] not love the world, neither the things of this world. If any man loves the world, the love of the Father is not in him." The experience of modern man demonstrates that it is more valuable to follow the older dispensation rather than the one from the so-called progressive revelation.

In the supposed inferior revelation, the observance of the sabbath was a fundamental hallmark of the Jews. It was the first in the list of holy seasons found in Lev. 26, the only one mentioned in the Decalogue (Exod. 20:8–11), and to be given a mythological basis (Gen. 2:2–3). Yet, in the so-called superior revelation, Jesus negates its sanctity by stating: "My Father has never ceased his work, and I am working too" (John 5:17–18). Which revelation is more humane: to allow men to rest from the hard work of the previous six days or to disregard the need for regenerating their energy and spirit?

The Jewish revelation demonstrates that although the ideas about God of the early Hebrews were primitive and anthropomorphic, these concepts eventually transform themselves into conceiving God as one incomparable in power, wisdom, mercy, goodness and holiness. No longer is God regarded as a man walking in the garden of Eden, attacking Moses like a demon because Moses had not circumcised his son, and killing the first-born of the Egyptians yet sparing those of the Israelites.

Contrast this moral journey with the shocking regression affected by the Christians. Backsliding to the very anthropomorphic and crude type of God the Jews had finally outgrown, the Christians merely poured new wine into old bottles—that God had begotten a Son who, while all the time retaining his divinity, was also truly man. Thus the cycle was completed: from a God conceived in terms of a man to a completely spiritual deity and back again to the God-man Jesus Christ!

There is more! What could be more revolting than a God who in Christ reconciles the world to himself (2 Cor. 5:19) by giving his only begotten Son (John 3:16) as the propitiation for our sins (1 John 4:20)? What a cruel and savage religion Christianity is in its need of a Father who requires a victim, the agonizing death of his only Son, before he can relinquish his vengeance on sinners whom he had made imperfect in the first place!

Enough said! "Progressive revelation" is doublespeak—to cover up the Christian devolution of religion!

# 24

# Suppose

Suppose you were down and out, and along came a stranger . . .
　　　Suppose he exuded charisma . . .

Suppose this man were already a proven leader with loyal followers . . .

Suppose this leader displayed a most unusual grasp of spirituality and insight . . .

Suppose he angrily denounced political leaders who were your oppressors . . .

Suppose he were the fulfillment of many Old Testament prophecies . . .

Suppose he were born of the union of a human woman and the Holy Spirit of God . . .

Suppose at his baptism God had publicly proclaimed to witnesses that he was his only Son . . .

Suppose this man promised you the kingdom of heaven . . .

Suppose he miraculously fed you, along with five thousand others, fish and bread when you were hungry . . .

Suppose he accomplished other miracles, like driving out demons and curing the blind and the lame . . .

Suppose he forgave you your sins . . .

Suppose he were the prophesied Messiah . . .

Wouldn't you unhesitatingly have followed such a god-man? Wouldn't you have done anything he asked of you?

Certainly you would have—and so would I!

But, if all of these marvelous things were true . . .

Why did this supposed god-man's friends think "he was out of his mind" (Mark 3:21)?

And why were his brothers, in another episode, still "not believers in him" (John 7:5)?

And why did "many of his disciples withdraw and no longer go about with him" (John 6:66)?

Do you suppose that all these wonderful "supposes" were just supposes so that his mother, brothers, and fallen away disciples were quite correct in their appraisal of Jesus?

# 25

# Capsule Arguments against Christ

Since its beginnings Christianity has used as one of its major polemical weapons the Old Testament as a mine for discovering prooftexts concerning its Messiah, Jesus Christ. This Christological basis is exemplified by reading what the *Scofield Reference Bible* states in its introduction: "The Central Theme of the Bible is Christ. It is this manifestation of Jesus Christ, his Person as 'God manifest in the flesh' . . . his sacrificial death, and his resurrection, which constitute the Gospel. Unto this *all preceding Scripture leads, from this all following Scripture proceeds*" (italics added).

If the whole Bible is about Jesus Christ, what better proof could the Christians have than to mine the Jewish Bible for prooftexts? They overlooked, however, those texts which *deny* that Jesus Christ is the Messiah and God. What follows are some of these counter prooftexts in capsule form. To play fair, I am taking them, with one exception, from the *Scofield Bible*.

The Old Testament explicitly warns against trusting in a man: "Thus saith the Lord, Cursed be the man that trusteth in man" (Jer. 17:5). Here is another: "Put not your trust in princes, nor in the son of man, in whom there is no help" (Ps. 146:3).

The Jewish Bible told Jews to punish a man who would claim to have a mother but no father. (This damaging statement is not in the *Scofield Bible*. It is, however, in the Jewish Publication Society's translation.) Here's the passage: "If . . . the son of thy mother . . . entice thee secretly, saying: 'Let us go and serve other gods' . . . thou shalt surely kill him" (Deut. 13:6–9).

The Old Testament said that any man who pretended to be divine would be humbled: "The lofty looks of man shall be humbled, and the haughtiness of man shall be bowed down, and the Lord alone shall be exalted . . ." (Isa. 2:11).

Moreover, Jesus could not have become immortal, and therefore he could not have become God. According to the account in the garden of Eden found in

85

Genesis, God did not want man to live forever: "And the Lord God said, Behold, the man is become one of us, to know good and evil: and now, lest he put forth his hand, and take also of the tree of life, and eat, and live forever. . . . Therefore the Lord God . . . drove out the man . . ." (Gen. 3:22–23).

Jesus, who called himself the Son of man, is to be completely ignored if we listen to the Old Testament: "Lord, what is a man, that thou takest knowledge of him! or the son of man, that thou makest account of him!" (Ps. 144:3).

The Old Testament also tells us that God recognizes no savior but himself: "I, even I, am the Lord; and beside me there is no savior" (Isa. 43:11).

By memorizing these capsule prooftexts, you can provide yourself with enough antidotes to ward off Christian claims about Jesus.

# 26

# Was Jesus Mr. Nice Guy?

Mildness, meekness, gentleness, and helpfulness is the image most have of Jesus. But was he Mr. Nice Guy? Let's see.

The Pharisees, pure and whole in their religious lives, protest to Jesus against his eating with tax collectors. Jesus answers them sarcastically, "Those who are well have no need of a physician, but those who are sick" (Luke 5:31).

Christ walked with his disciples in the fields during the sabbath. They plucked corn as they made their way, thereby violating the ban on working on the holy day. For this they were rebuked by the Pharisees. Instead of conforming like a loyal Jew, Jesus storms back at them: "The sabbath was made for man, not man for the sabbath" (Mark 2:27).

In reply to his mother and brothers who stood outside a synagogue waiting to speak to Jesus who was inside lecturing, he shocked everyone by denying that his family were God-fearing, shouting: " 'Who is my mother and brothers?' And stretching his hand toward his disciples, he said: 'For whoever does the will of my Father in heaven is my brother and sister and mother' " (Matt. 12:48–49).

On one occasion, Jesus flouts a most important religious law, that of carefully caring for the dead. A disciple had made a most reasonable request, "Lord, let me first go and bury my father." But Jesus excoriates him: "Leave the dead to bury their own dead; but as for you, go and proclaim the kingdom of God" (Luke 9:59–60).

Again he rebuffed another disciple who had said: "I will follow you Lord; but let me first say farewell to those at home." Jesus admonished him: "No one who puts his hand to the plow and looks back is fit for the kingdom of God" (Luke 9:61–62).

When Jesus flushes the Temple of moneychangers, he thunders: "It is written, 'My house shall be a house of prayer;' but you have made it a den of robbers" (Luke 19:39–40).

After Peter made his great confession that Jesus was indeed the Christ, Jesus began to teach his disciples that he must suffer, be killed and, after three days, rise again. Peter could not believe this and rebuked Jesus for exaggerating. Spewing venom at his chief disciple, Jesus said: "Get behind me, Satan! For you are not on the side of God, but of men" (Mark 8:29–33).

On the day that his band came from Bethany, Jesus became hungry. Seeing in the distance a fig tree in leaf, he went to see if there was any fruit. Finding nothing but leaves, for it was not the season for figs, Jesus condemned it: "May no one ever eat fruit from you again" (Mark 11:12–14). "And the fig tree withered at once" (Matt. 21:19).

When some disciples complained about Jesus wasting a great deal of money because he allowed a woman to pour very expensive ointment over his head, he blasted them: "Let her alone; why do you trouble her? She has done a beautiful thing to me. For you will always have the poor with you, and wherever you will, you can do good to them; but you will not always have me" (Mark 14:6–8).

Let's not forget these punishing words from Jesus: "If a man does not abide in me, he is cast forth as a branch and withers; and the branches are gathered, thrown into the fire and burned" (John 15:6).

Finally, "But as for these enemies of mine, who did not want me to reign over them, bring them here and slay them before me" (Luke 19:27).

Was Jesus really Mr. Nice Guy?

# 27

# Jesus the Sinner

According to Christian theology, Jesus Christ was not simply a messenger from God like the Old Testament prophets. Rather, he was the "eternal Son of God taking on human nature, yet free from any taint of sin" (2 Cor. 5:21; 1 Pet. 2:22; 1 John 3:5). As a God-man, he had both a divine and a human nature united in one person. Any objective reading of the Gospels will prove this to be an outlandish lie!

To demonstrate the shocking falsity of Jesus' actual behavior when compared to his pious mouthings, I will sketch some brief episodes from his life and then compare them to his own statements.

In the Gospel according to John, Jesus excoriates a group of Jews "who had believed in him." Here are Jesus' own words: "You are of your father the devil. . . . He was a murderer from the beginning . . . he is a . . . liar . . . and the father of lies" (John 8:44–45).

Doesn't this passage drip with hatred, for Jesus is equating the God of the Jews with the Devil, a murderer and a liar?

Does this not illustrate the sinful hypocrisy of Jesus who said that the first great commandment was to "love your God with all your heart, and with all your soul, and with all your mind" (Matt. 22:37)?

In another episode, recorded in the twenty-third chapter of Matthew, we hear the scathing words of Jesus to the scribes and Pharisees (who were the pillars of Jewish society): "Woe to you . . . hypocrites . . . blind guides . . . whitewashed tombs . . . serpents . . . brood of vipers . . ." plus a few other unsavory epithets like "killers" and "crucifiers."

This was not just an isolated incident, for Jesus does not hesitate to ream his chief disciple Peter by calling him Satan and a hindrance (Matt. 16:23).

Compare this to Jesus' command as recorded in the very same Matthean Gospel: "And the second [great commandment] is, you shall love your neighbor as yourself" (22:19). As defined by Jesus himself, weren't his curses of the scribes, Pharisees, and his chief disciple sins?

Found also in Matthew 23:17 is his criticism of the scribes and Pharisees: "You blind fools!" Yet, when we examine the supposed sweetness and light of his Sermon on the Mount in Matthew's account, we discover another sinful utterance, for Jesus plainly states: "Whoever says, 'You fool!' shall be liable to the hell of fire" (5:22).

When one of Jesus' disciples asked if he could "first go and bury [his] father," Jesus replied: "Follow me, and leave the dead to bury their own dead" (Matt. 8:22).

And when Jesus' mother and brothers came to take him home he verbally disowned them (Mark 3:34–35).

These two episodes are in utter contradiction to Jesus' acceptance of the Ten Commandments: "You know the commandments: . . . Honor your mother and father" (Mark 10:19). Wasn't Jesus' treatment of his mother sinful?

Finally, what better proof do we need than the very admission of Jesus himself: "Why do you call me good? No one is good but God alone" (Mark 10:18).

Thus, we have demonstrated with a mere handful of illustrations that this supposed God-man was, contrary to all Christian confessions, as great a sinner as most humans!

# 28

# Jesus and the Ten Commandments:
# How Many Did He Break?

**B**orn of Jewish parents, circumcised as all Jewish males had to be, preaching in Jewish houses of worship, raising Cain with money-lenders whom he thought were desecrating his Father's Temple—all demonstrate the reputed "Jewishness" of Jesus. But how "Jewish" was he? Did he follow the one true path to righteousness laid down by the great lawgiver Moses? Or did he willfully decide not to walk in the footsteps of his people's preeminent prophet? One litmus test is to see if Jesus adhered to the Ten Commandments.

Taking these from Exodus 20, we find the first commandment is: "You shall have no other gods before me." If this means that no other spiritual entities other than God himself is to be recognized, let alone worshiped, then Jesus is guilty of disobeying this overriding injunction. Such an interpretation is not at all argumentative. Turn to the forty-fourth chapter of Isaiah and you will discover that this most authoritative prophet not only heaps the most caustic ridicule on the makers and worshipers of idols but also insists that God himself is the first and last and that there is no God beside him. This means that there is no one else but God who can save (Isa. 43:3, 7, 11, 14), and that there is no other author but God of both good and evil (Exod. 4:11; Isa. 45:7).

By the Jews acknowledging that God is the only source of good and evil, they have eliminated the enigma and inherent contradiction of dualism which Jesus was unwilling to do. For we find many scenes and sayings of Jesus in which this repugnant dualism is plainly brought out. For instance, Jesus has a confrontation with Satan in Matthew 4; rebukes Satan in Matthew 17; tells his disciples they have power over devils in Luke 10; admits that there are children of the "Wicked One" in Matthew 13; berates Peter his chief disciple by calling him "Satan" in Mark 8; and castigates Judas the informant as a devil in John 6. What else, on the witness provided by the Gospels themselves, can we conclude than that Jesus did not agree to the unity, or oneness, of God, and thus violated the first commandment.

Now let us go to the commandment "Remember the Sabbath day, to keep it holy." Jesus refused to obey this, instead calling himself "the Lord of the sabbath" (Matt. 12:8). He even presumes to state that because his Father works on the Sabbath, then so does he (John 5:17). It is clear that Jesus defied his Father by repudiating this commandment.

We next come to the commandment "You shall not kill." Although Jesus never killed anyone while he was alive, he certainly made many threats that he would do so at some future time. In Matt. 10:34 Jesus emphasizes: "Do not think that I have come to bring peace, but a sword. For I came to set man against his father. . . ." And in the same chapter (10:15), Jesus predicts: "Truly, I say to you, it shall be more tolerable on the day of judgment for the land of Sodom and Gomorrah than for that town." Revelation 17:14 assures us: "These shall make war with the Lamb (Jesus) and the Lamb shall overcome them." The carnage of the death-dealing "Word of God" becomes overwhelming in Rev. 19:13–21. Because of these texts we must conclude that Jesus violated this prohibition.

That Jesus could not plead innocence for not knowing all of the Ten Commandments is easily dispelled because Jesus admitted that he *did* know them. In Mark 10:19, Jesus himself lists six of the Commandments to a questioner who wanted to know what he had to do to inherit perpetual life.

The conclusion is obvious. Jesus abrogated and disobeyed at least four of God's most authoritative commandments, making him a sinner.

# 29

# The Fear and Cowardice of God

It is claimed that Jesus Christ is God. Here is why.

Doubting Thomas calls Jesus "My God," and is rebuked for not believing it before: "And Thomas answered and said to him [Jesus], 'My Lord and my God' " (John 20:28).

"Behold, a virgin shall be with child, and shall bring forth a son, and they shall call his name Emmanuel, which means God is with us" (Matt. 1:23).

". . . looking forward to the happy fulfillment of our hope when the splendor of our great God and Savior Christ Jesus will appear" (Titus 2:13).

So if Jesus were God, it should follow that he had nothing to fear from mere mortal man. But was he fearless? Or was he a coward?

"And Jesus said to him [whose leprosy was healed], 'See that you say nothing to anyone . . .'" (Matt. 8:4). Why the great secrecy? Was Jesus afraid that he would be picked up by the Temple police and punished?

The next text says: "But the Pharisees went out and took counsel against him, how to destroy him. Jesus aware of this, withdrew from there. And many followed him, and he healed all, and ordered them not to make him known" (Matt. 12:14–16). Once again, Jesus shows his fear.

"The Pharisees went out, and immediately held counsel with the Herodians against him, how to destroy him. Jesus withdrew with his disciples to the sea. . . . And he told his disciples to have a boat ready for him because of the crowd, lest they should crush him" (Mark 3:6–9).

"After this Jesus went about in Galilee; he would not go about in Judea, because the Jews sought to kill him" (John 7:1).

"About the ninth hour Jesus cried out in a loud voice, 'Eli, Eli, lema sabachthani?' that is, 'My God, my God, why have you forsaken me?'" (Matt. 27:46).

"They wanted to arrest him, but he eluded them" (John 10:39).

"At this they picked up stones to throw at him; but Jesus hid himself and left the Temple" (John 8:59).

"When they heard this in the synagogue, everyone was enraged. They sprang to their feet and hustled him out of town; and they took him up to the brow of the hill their town was built on, intending to throw him down the cliff, but he slipped through the crowd and walked away" (Luke 4:28–30).

No matter what you think of the God of the Old Testament, he was one to fear, not one who was afraid!

# 30

# Jesus and the Dagger Men

Read the first four verses of Luke 13. Do you know what it means when the text tells us about "the Galileans whose blood Pilate had mingled with their sacrifices," and "those eighteen upon whom the Tower of Siloam fell and killed?"

The answer will show that Jesus had among his closest companions at least two revolutionists; and that he himself had the same attitude as a revolutionary. They were known as Zealots, or Sicarii (dagger men).

There was his chief disciple, Simon bar-Jona, known to us as Simon Peter or just plain Peter. It was upon this "rock" that, according to the Roman Catholic Church, Jesus founded his church (Matt. 16:15–19).

Biblical scholar Oscar Cullman says that "bar-Jona" ordinarily meant "son of Jonah," but this form was not generally used in the Holy Land. Instead the Jews attached a different meaning, one taken from the Akkadian "barjona" which they then used as a synonym for "terrorist."

We know that Peter was a violent man, for it was he who drew his sword and cut off the ear of the high priest's slave during the betrayal of Jesus by Judas in the garden on the Mount of Olives (John 18:10–11).

The other disciple in Jesus' inner circle was Simon the Canaanite, also called Simon the Zealot (Matt. 10:4; Luke 6:15; Acts 1:13). These two Zealots were, of course, part of the band which accompanied Jesus on his mission to Jerusalem.

When Jesus decided to campaign in the Holy City, he wanted to know what people thought of him.

Who did people say he was, he asked his disciples one day?

They answered: some said he was John the Baptist come back to life, others that he was Elijah, still others that he was one of the prophets.

But you, who do you say I am, interrupted Jesus? It was then that Peter spoke the words that would prove fatal to the Master: "Thou art the Messiah, the son of the living God. Thou art he who is destined to liberate the people of Israel" (Matt. 16:13–16).

Jesus was startled by Peter's bold language. He commanded his disciples, who had heard Peter's confession, to tell this to no one. But the effect on Jesus was tremendous. For he suddenly saw himself in this new light. Peter's confession seems to have transformed Jesus' perception of his own mission.

When Peter had made his impetuous declaration, the band was already on the road to Jerusalem. They were, however, no longer a handful of just twelve disciples, for a few hundred men had by now attached themselves to the party.

These were patriots, fishermen, peasants, and Zealots—the feared Sicarii who hated the ruling tyrants and who knew how to wield a knife or sword when needed.

Very large crowds had gathered when Jesus, according to Matthew's Gospel, came into the city. He rode in on a donkey just as "a son of David" would have, as a descendent of the most illustrious and warlike dynasty in Jewish history. The people did not mistake the intention of the entry. For they spread their garments, something that was not done when a rabbi or teacher, no matter how beloved or renowned, came into town. Moreover, they shouted "Hosanna," a messianic acclamation.

There the story ends. Nothing more is heard of that stirring entry which Christians celebrate as Palm Sunday. Neither the Roman authorities nor the Jewish leaders seemed to have paid the least attention to that messianic procession. Why does Matthew break off the story? Because Jesus, or those in his circle, or both, aimed at nothing less than an insurrection. They came for the same purpose as past and future messianic movements did—to crush the occupying enemy so as to regain national independence. Matthew suppresses further details because not only did Jesus fail in his mission but because he also wanted to convince the Roman authorities that the founder and followers of Christianity were *not* revolutionaries. Since Jesus' mission was stopped by the aggressive response of the Roman legionnaires, Matthew had to save the situation by making it seem that his Master was innocent as a lamb, and who did not himself know why he was led before Pilate for crucifixion.

By suppressing this truth, Christians were free to move about and to propagandize and grow. The truth would have shown that Jesus was not a God-man, but only too human. For the Romans in this part of their empire already had too much experience with upstart messianic movements.

Even before Jesus' time, during the reign of Archelous, messianic Zealots had attempted a coup by marching boldly into Jerusalem with the intention of occupying the dominant positions.

"Zealot" is the name recorded by the Jewish historian Josephus for some Jewish resistance fighters in the Jewish war against the Romans (66–73 C.E.). The original meaning of Zealots comes from associating them with the kind of religious fervor that recalls the Phineas in Num. 25:7–13.

Here Phineas is praised for his "zeal" in resorting to violent action in defending the honor of God. The incident involved an Israelite who, in direct disregard of God's command to leave the Moabite women and their phallic god Baal Peor alone, was caught by Phineas having sexual intercourse with a Moabite woman in his tent. With great moral indignation, Phineas speared both of them through their genitals while they were in coition. Phineas indeed was a zealot for God.

The Zealots were described by Josephus as brigands or Sicarii. He blamed them for the catastrophe of 70 C.E. In his book *Antiquities,* this former Jewish general records that a Zealot, a Galilean named Judah, incited his countrymen to revolt, upbraiding them as cowards for consenting to pay tribute to the Romans and for tolerating mortal masters instead of holding fast to God as their Lord. He goes on to tell us that Judah was a sophist who founded a sect of his own, having little in common with the others, that is, the Pharisees, Sadducees, and Essenes.

Josephus says further that the followers of Judah reluctantly associated themselves generally with the Pharisees, and that "they have a passion for liberty that is almost unconquerable, since they are convinced that God is their leader and master."

What happened to Judah? Josephus does not tell us but the New Testament book of Acts does. There it says that Judah perished in the suppression of the revolt of 6 C.E. (Acts 5:37). The survivors of this movement took to the deserts where they maintained a guerrilla resistance to the Romans. The fact that Jesus chose two Zealots as apostles reveals that this party was well known in Galilee about 28 C.E.

It was these Galilean Zealots who came with Jesus on his messianic entry into Jerusalem and who were met head-on and lambasted by Roman soldiers. Blocked in their initial coup, these followers of Jesus withdrew to the Mount of Olives, there to reassemble and plan further action.

Their chief problem was how to get into the closely guarded city. So we must ask: how did the band of Zealots get into the Temple? The same way the army of modern Israel in 1949 defeated greatly superior Egyptian forces which had invaded the Negeb. They used a forgotten Roman road through the desert allowing them to attack a surprised enemy from the rear. By a similar strategy king David long before had captured the Citadel of Jerusalem from the Jebusites.

David had already been king for seven years in Hebron, while Jerusalem was still in the hands of the original Canaanite inhabitants. Neither Joshua, the successor of Moses, nor any other of the Israelite tribal chiefs after him, had ever been able to expel the Jebusites from their mighty citadel on Mount Moriah.

The second book of Samuel (5:7–8) tells how David accomplished this feat: he went through the watercourse! He entered the aqueduct at the Tower of Siloam and proceeded underground until he was right in the heart of the Jebusite fortress.

The very same tactic was decided upon by these Galilean hotheads. As they burst out of the watercourse and began taking over the strong points in the Temple area, Pilate's soldiers counterattacked. The Zealots were soon trapped. Instead of taking his prisoners outside the sacred precincts to have them crucified, the Procurator commanded his men to lead the captives upstairs. There they were slaughtered, by order of Pilate, and their blood—as the New Testament says—was mingled with the blood of the bullock being sacrificed by the priest.

Still, that was not the end of the bloody affair. Some of the Zealots had managed to retreat back into the watercourse. They emerged at the end of the tunnel, inside the Tower of Siloam. There they overpowered the sentinels and established themselves.

As soon as Pilate learned that the Tower of Siloam was in the hands of the insurrectionists, he brought up battering rams to attack the place. The Siloam bastion was battered to pieces. After a few days the walls collapsed, burying the Zealots under the ruins. As the New Testament says: "eighteen fell and were killed" (Luke 13:14).

Two of the Zealot leaders were crucified a few days later, one on the right side, the other on his left of Jesus. For the New Testament says specifically that they were "under the condemnation," that is, under the same sentence for the same crime as Jesus. One of them cried to their leader Jesus: "Art thou not the Messiah? Save thyself and us" (Luke 23:39). These very natural questions show that the speaker was not a robber or a common criminal, as has usually been held by Christian apologists, but that the Zealot dagger men knew very well what the situation was.

Jesus refers to these Zealot ambitions when he says that the kingdom of heaven "has been coming violently" and "men of violence will take it by force" (Matt. 11:12).

In Luke 22:36 Jesus tells his disciples "who have no sword to sell their mantle and buy one."

Finally, Jesus acknowledges that he was one of the law breakers, because he says: "For I tell you that this scripture must be fulfilled in me: 'And he was reckoned with transgressors [he's quoting Isa. 53:12]'; for what is written about me has its fulfillment" (Luke 22:37).

# 31

# Guess Who?

Let's see if you can recognize this famous character. I'm going to give you a large number of clues to make it easy for you. But before we begin, I want to make a gentlemen's bet that you'll guess wrong. Now, no cheating.

1. _____ was born of the Virgin Mary, who conceived him without carnal intercourse.

2. The incarnation of _____ is recorded to have been brought about by the descent of the divine power called the Holy Ghost upon the Virgin Mary.

3. The birth of _____ was announced by the "Messianic Star."

4. The infant _____ was presented with costly jewels and precious substances.

5. _____ the son of Mary was said to have been born on Christmas day.

6. _____ was a child in danger, his life being threatened by a king who was advised to kill the child.

7. When he was twelve years old, _____ was taken to the Temple where he astounded everyone with his knowledge.

8. The ancestry of _____ is traced from his father through various individuals of royalty.

9. When _____ was about to start his mission, the Devil appeared in order to tempt him.

10. _____ would not listen to the words of the Evil One, after which _____ fasted for a long time.

11. _____ the Savior, was baptized by the Holy Ghost.

12. On one occasion, near the end of his life, _____ is reported to have been "transfigured" while on a mountain.

13. _____ performed great miracles for the benefit of mankind.

14. By prayers in the name of_____, his followers expect to receive the rewards of paradise.

15. After _____ died and was buried, the cloth coverings of his body fell away, and his tomb was opened by supernatural powers.

16. _____ ascended bodily to the celestial regions after his mission on earth was fulfilled.

17. _____ is to come back to earth again to restore order and happiness.

18. _____ is to be the judge of the dead.

19. _____ is the Alpha and Omega, without beginning or end, the "Supreme Being."

20. _____ is represented as saying: "Let all the sins that were committed in this world fall on me, that the world may be delivered."

21. _____ was described as a superhuman organ of light to whom a superhuman organ of darkness was opposed.

22. _____ came not to destroy the law but to fulfil it. He represented himself as one link in a long chain of enlightened teachers.

23. The motive for all our actions according to _____ should be pity or love for our neighbor.

24. During the early part of his career as a teacher, _____ delivered a discourse after which some of listeners became his disciples.

25. Those who became _____ disciples were told they must renounce the world, give up all their riches, and avow poverty.

26. When _____ time on earth was about to end, he, foreseeing all things that would happen in the future, instructed his disciples that he would always be with them.

27. _____ was to establish a religious kingdom—"a kingdom of heaven."

28. _____ said: "Though the heavens were to fall to earth and the great world were to be swallowed up and pass away, be assured that my words are true."

29. _____ said: "There is no passion more violent than voluptuousness. Beware of fixing your eyes upon women. If you find yourself in their company, let it be as if you were not present."

30. _____ knew the thoughts of others.

Well? Who is it? Remember our gentlemen's agreement—no cheating. I bet you thought you had the answer right off. No, it's *not* Jesus Christ.

The famous character just described is Buddha! No two legendary histories of characters with so much mythology as part of their biographies resemble each other more than Jesus and Buddha. Since Buddha precedes Jesus by five hundred years, as late-comers Christians must have copied extensively from the Buddhists! This speaks volumes, telling us that contrary to their claims Christianity was hardly unique.

# THE MEANING OF
# CHRISTIAN SYMBOLS

# 32

# Twice-Born

Did you know that every time you entered a church you were reborn? Yes, you're reborn whether you want to be or not. For that is the very function of the church's architecture, it being modeled on a woman's genitals. Every time you go through the door, you must realize that you are reentering the womb, and thus are born again and again.

The church is not unique in this respect. The female characteristic of the house of God goes back to prehistory. Dig out your Old Testament and carefully reread the twenty-sixth chapter of Exodus. This is a detailed description of the Tent of Meeting or Tabernacle. The great tent was to have a covering of goat's skins, of "ram's skins died red," and of "badger's skins." (This reference to "badger's" is a mistranslation and should be "dolphin's skins.")

In any case, these coverings are so drawn over at one end that they meet in a closed slit through which the high priest must dramatically force his way during the great festival. If you care to draw the result with colored crayon you would draw an inner layer of fine skins, and around this sheepskin dyed red, and around this the hairy goat skins, all of which portray a most illuminating phallic picture!

Inside the tent was the ark, and upon it rested a slab of gold, the "mercy seat." At each end of the mercy-seat were two winged figures, golden cherubs. Cherubs are mentioned in Exod. 25:19.

Contrary to the commandment against "graven images," these cherubs were prominent in the Temple ritual right down to the end of the second Jewish commonwealth (70 C.E.). Furthermore, in their final version the cherubim depicted two snakes in sexual embrace, an elaborate gift to the Jerusalem Temple from the rich Jews of Alexandria—an erotic representation which was considered obscene by the pagans when they finally had a chance to look at them. So we have here a most striking physical visual image of the phallicism practiced by the Jews after the time of Christ!

103

Many of the other ritual furnishings like the ark, menorah, the altar with horns, the special robe of the high priest with pomegranates along its bottom—all are of phallic significance. For now only the structure of the tent of meeting is important.

Let me now go on to describe the structure of the Christian church. When you enter you pass through a double door. These stand for the "labia majora," or "greater lips"—two narrow folds of tissue which form the outside boundaries of the vulva. These doors are painted red in many churches, as they should be because the color represents the life-giving blood of the female.

Going farther inside, you must pass through another double door, the "labia minora," or "lesser lips"—two narrow folds of tissue enclosed within the cleft of the labia majora. The labia minora are also called "nympha."

When you reach the interior or auditorium, you are now in the "womb."

On each side of the altar you can observe doors which lead into rooms; these are the "Fallopian tubes"—those slender ducts that connect the uterus to the region of each of the ovaries.

In these rooms the candidate for baptism comes into contact with the priest or preacher and receives the "seed of regeneration." Then when he comes back to the altar he is baptized—that is to say he is cleansed with "amniotic fluid," the watery liquid contained in the sac in which the embryo is suspended.

The altar is the "membrum virile," the "penis erectus," or the firm, upright male member.

Thus you have both necessary reproductive organs symbolically represented for rebirth. The person who then exits the church is now believed to have a reborn soul!

Overelaborate as this may seem, it does not differ from the practice in many ancient and a few modern religions where the devotees pass through yoni-shaped holes, or clefts in stone slabs, for the purpose of becoming either fruitful or born-again, or of becoming cleansed of their sins.

Yoni-shaped openings have been reproduced in the many elliptically shaped windows which adorn churches, their doors, and other openings. Dozens of well-known paintings of the Virgin Mary and of Jesus have an ellipse around them, in many cases quite a suggestive one. In Utrecht there is a picture of Elizabeth and Mary, painted around 1400 C.E., showing Jesus and John the Baptist as embryos enclosed in ellipses. This kind of representation proves beyond all doubt that the ellipse was recognized as the yoni or "door of life."

In Dumblane Abbey there is a window which was considered by the famous art critic Ruskin to be the most beautiful in England. It is quite realistic in its symbolism, showing the yoni and all its component parts: the labia majora, labia minora, clitoris, vestibule, and orifice.

Until this century you could find Shela-na-Gigs either over or alongside the entrances to churches. Since a Shela-na-Gig was a bas relief of a woman shown spreading her yoni, this was a clear meaning of the building.

So if you want to be cleansed of your sins or be reborn, enter a church. Better still, simply pass through any hole in a tree or a stone pillar with a hole.

# 33

# The Trinity

Let's get one thing straight at the start: there is absolutely no mention in the earliest New Testament manuscripts of the Trinity. God the Father, yes; Jesus his Son, certainly; the Holy Ghost, of course. But all separately, and in no way as the theological formula dreamed up by the Council of Nicea. The texts which purportedly stated the Trinitarian formula that was found in Matt. 16:9 and 1 John 5:8 are well recognized by scholars as "interpolations" and by laymen as "pious lies."

Jesus never mentioned such a coequal Trinity; and the earliest Christians did not apply it to their own faith. Even the Apostle's Creed, the earliest formula of the Christian faith, knows nothing of it. The concept was only adopted by the Church three hundred years after the death of Jesus. So where did it come from?

The conception is entirely pagan! In the fourth century B.C.E., Aristotle wrote in *On The Heavens*, "All things are three, and thrice is all; for, as the Pythagoreans say, everything and all things are bounded by threes, for the end, the middle, and the beginning have this number in everything, and these compose the number of the Trinity."

We can add to this, tracing the concept back to the early Egyptians and through the caravan and sea routes to ancient India. The Egyptian influence on succeeding religious thought was permanent. They usually arranged their gods and goddesses in trinities: Osiris, Isis, and Horus; Amen, Mut, and Khonsu. Brahman, Siva, and Vishnu of Hindu fame are another example of a trinity.

Plutarch relates that Ahura Mazda, the supreme god of the Persians, "thrice multiplied himself." Mithra was the son of Ahura, yet was Ahura himself, much like Jesus is the Son yet God himself.

The Chinese Taoists worshiped a self-created trinity having three attributes which Lao-tse called "I-He-Wei," a term almost identical with the sound used to pronounce "Yahweh," the God of the Old Testament. When preceded by the title "Adonai," Yahweh is pronounced Ye Ho Wih.

The name of Yahweh was also represented by the *tenth* number of the Hebrew alphabet, "Yod." The reason is intriguing, giving us a glimpse into the window of phallicism—an in-word for sex worship.

In the language of symbolism, everything created which resembles its Creator was used to symbolize that Creator. Since the gods everywhere were anthropomorphic—made in the image of man—their symbols ran the gamut from the most realistic portrayals of the lingam (male sexual organ) and yoni (the female counterpart) to the most abstract.

The most refined symbol of the male member was an upright shaft or pillar; a mere circle or oval stood for the female. In this simple combination, then, the pillar—or "1"—joined with the yoni—"0"—may be read as "10" or the number ten. It follows that Yahweh was the magic, phallic number ten ("10").*

Another fitting symbol expressing God's male essence was the form of a cross using the letter "tau" or "T." This is a streamlined "T." If you round the ends of the horizontal bar into loops, making them much like testicles, you will have drawn the original tau.

In its Ethiopian form, the tau ("T") is the exact forerunner of the Christian cross. Proselytes of Mithra were marked on their foreheads with the tau. At Eleusis, initiates were marked with this sign before they were admitted to the Mysteries. According to the Vulgate translation of Ezek. 9:4, the ancient form of the Hebrew "T" was stamped on the foreheads of those men of Judah who feared the Lord.

This threefold character of the male symbol was overarching in importance because all of the creative gods of antiquity were personifications of the genital powers: the left testicle, the right testicle, and the upright penis in between were arranged as a group of three—in other words, a trinity.

By the time the Christians came on the scene, the trinity had become the symbol par excellence. It merged the idea of man's new birth in this world by his Creator with that of his everlasting life in the next by the ransomed God-man Christ. The symbols of the "tau," "T," "cross," and "trinity" fitted together like Chinese boxes.

It looked like an easy and natural acquisition for the new Christian religion. Natural it was, but its adoption was long and bitter. Since the Christians as yet had no prooftext in their sacred works for the trinity, belligerent clerics chose sides and drew verbal and real blood.

The war, brewing for four long centuries, finally exploded when an Egyptian Christian cleric named Arius challenged the growing forces touting the Trinity. If Christ had been begotten by the Father, argued Arius, this had to have taken

---

*The correlation between letters and numbers goes back, as far as we know, to the Pythagoreans and their mysticism regarding numbers. This mysticism was absorbed by just about every culture. Cabala (or Kabala) is based upon it. See Robert Graves, *The White Goddess: A Historical Grammar of Poetic Myth* (New York: Creative Age Press, 1948), and Ernest Busenbark, *Symbols, Sex, and the Stars in Popular Beliefs* (New York: Truth Seeker Co., 1949).

place over time. First in time, and therefore first in authority, he continued, had to be the Father; then came Jesus Christ his Son. Thus Christ (or the Logos) could not be coequal, coeternal, or of the exact substance as God the Father. Therefore, Christ was inferior to the Father. To pour salt into the wound, Arius declared that since the Holy Ghost was begotten by the Logos, it was even less than the Logos!

Although most of his declarations harmonized with the early Pauline as well as with second-century theology, it had by now become blasphemy. Arius's bishop was so shocked that he called a council to unfrock the honest cleric. Followers, however, came flocking to the side of Arius. According to the Church historian Eusebius, the controversy made the cities of the Empire ring with "such tumult and disorder . . . that the Christian religion afforded a subject of profane merriment to the pagans, even in their theaters."

The Arians were promptly challenged by another Alexandrian, Athenasius. Coming from Egypt—remember it was permeated with the idea of trinities— Athenasius acted as a theological sword, making it clear that if Christ and the Holy Ghost were not of the same substance as the Father, then polytheism would triumph.

The warring parties, hurling anathemas at each other, gained and lost the field several times. Athenasius and his Trinitarians finally won the crucial battle.

Christendom is still plagued with the consequences. The Eastern part of the Church broke from the West, partly because it held that the Holy Ghost emanated from the Father only. Protestant sects like the original Unitarians further splintered the Western See. Worst of all, a dogma was imposed which completely defied reason, making Christianity a laughingstock among rational people, and compelling the rest to live with this aberration.

# 34

# The Fish Head

The ceremonial headdress worn by the pope is called a "miter," but just as well could have been named "the Fish Head" because it originally represented the open mouth of the fish god. It is a tall, ornamented hat with peaks in front and back and is worn as a mark of the pope's high office.

It so happens that this "fish head" hat has a long and interesting history, for it started out as the symbol of the great Babylonian god Ea. In the Babylonian pantheon, the water god Ea ruled over the slimy waters of the great deep out of which the world was formed. In token of this tradition, a large basin of water called "apsu" was kept in all Babylonian temples. These represented the waste of waters, and was very much like the description given in the first chapter of Genesis.

Ancient myths represent Ea as a friendly god who rose out of the sea each morning to teach agriculture, civil government, handicrafts and other arts needed by civilization. In early sculpture he is portrayed as a merman—half man, half fish.

In later versions Ea appears as the fish god Dagon to whom the Philistines built temples of worship. According to the Old Testament, they set up temples in Gaza (Judg. 16:33) and Ashdod (1 Sam. 5:1–7). These Philistines originated as mercenaries, possibly brought to Canaan by Ramses III after his victory over them. They established their own rule there after the collapse of Egyptian sovereignty in Canaan. After the battle at Mount Gilboa against the Israelites, the Philistines exposed the body of Saul, the Israelite's first king and predecessor of David, at their temple of Dagon.

Further proof of the Dagon cult in Canaan is found in the names of the two settlements at Beth-Dagon (Josh. 15:41, 19:27). A third is mentioned by Sennacherib as one of his conquests in his third campaign against the West which included Judah.

When that portion of Semites who later became known as the Israelites finally broke the yoke of the Philistines under king David (c.1000 B.C.E.), their own culture had already assimilated much of their enemy's religion. (In fact, 1 Sam. 27 tells us that David learned much of his fighting tactics as a mercenary under the Philistines.)

Part of the Israelite assimilation consisted of imitating the Philistine priest who, to incarnate himself as the god Dagon, dressed himself with the skin of a fish, placing the fish's open-mouthed head upon his own, just as the pope wears his miter. One of the commandments of Yahweh, given in Exodus 28, is for the high priest Aaron to wear such a fish head as his official headdress!

Besides the high priest wearing Dagon's fish head, there are other important connections with the fish cult. The great successor to Moses was named "Joshua son of Nun," which means "Joshua of the Fish." Another of his names, surprisingly, was "the Savior," or in Hebrew "Joshua," or in its hellenized form "Jesus"! The Great Fish, Leviathan, was in fact regarded by the Jews as the Messiah, or Christ, whose true name was Ji-Nun.

Dagon is also identified with the second person of the Sumerian and Babylonian trinities as Tammuz the Only-begotten Son, or Adonis the Lord, another dying and resurrected god like Jesus Christ.

The fish was, therefore, among the early Christians the common emblem of Jesus Christ. This was explained by an ingenious anagram. After condemning the error of those heretical Christians who regarded Christ as a serpent, the early Church Father Tertullian says: "But we, little fishes, followers of our fish, Jesus Christ, are born of water, nor can we otherwise obtain eternal salvation."

In accordance with these ideas, the Jews developed a custom of eating sacramental meals consisting of fish, thereby eating the substance of the divine Messiah. As such, this Messiah was said not only to be food for his believers but also to provide fertility for those who ate him. The custom about fish being food for all is found in the Gospel miracle about the multiplication of the two fish.

Fish were in fact the usual ingredient in the eucharistic meal in the early Church and were also represented in early Christian pictography. This custom survived until recently by Catholics eating fish on Fridays. Why Fridays? Because, among almost all cultures, fish were believed to impart fertility. For this reason they were not only sacred to Aphrodite but to the Nordic goddess Frigga—from whom we have derived the name for our "Friday!"

Earlier it was pointed out that Ea, or Dagon, was the water god and that the "deep" out of which the world was created was symbolized by a large basin kept in all Babylonian temples. This connects up with the rite of baptism preached by John the Baptist and continued by those Christians who followed his rival Jesus, coming down the centuries from the old Sumerian temple city Eridu, home of the water god Ea.

His symbol was the original Aquarius—the water bearer of the zodiac. This is the sign into which the sun enters in the winter solstice for rebirth. In the Hellenistic period, Ea was called "Oannes," which in Greek is "Ioannes," in Latin "Johannes," in Hebrew "Yohanan," and in English "John." Several scholars have therefore suggested that there never was a John or Jesus, but only a water god Oannes and a sun god Jesus.

So the next time you see the pope or cardinal wearing his fish-head hat, do not think of him not as a modern clergyman, but as an ancient Sumerian-Babylonian-Philistinian-Jewish priest performing his rites and vocalizing his myths for the hoary god Ea-Tammuz-Dagon-Yahweh!

# JEWS, CATHOLICS, AND FUNDAMENTALIST PROTESTANTS

# 35

# Monotheism:
# Breeder of Intolerance,
# Destruction, and Genocide

Christian Fundamentalists are dogmatically positive they have their hands on the "truth." They have been prodded from their sleep and, like the provoked Jesus found in Revelation, are now energetically forging thunderbolts to put the fear of God in us. They are absolutely sure we are going to hell if we do not accept their religious views on right-to-life rather than abortion, school prayer rather than separation of church and state, creationism rather than evolution, and a host of other no-nos in their agenda.

Where do these crustaceous Christians get their intolerant and destructive attitudes? Why, from the monotheism of the Jews! These people over their long history gradually separated their worship of God from the worship of nature. As nature receded, their God grew more important until he was almost divorced from his creation, becoming nature's supreme craftsman—the potter in control yet separated from his handiwork.

With the growth of the one-God concept (monotheism) came the terrible concomitants of intolerance and the commandments to destroy the sacred items of other worshipers, going so far as to destroy those who believed in many gods (polytheism). The justification for this is found in Exod. 23:23–24: "When my angel goes before you, and brings you into the Amorites, and the Hittites, and the Perizzites, and the Canaanites, the Hivites, and the Jebusites, and I blot them out, you shall not bow down to their gods, nor serve them, nor do according to their works, but you shall *utterly overcome* them and break their pillars in pieces. . . . You shall serve the Lord your God, and I will bless your bread . . ." (italics added).

This is reinforced by Exod. 34:13–14: "You shall tear down their altars, and smash their sacred pillars, and cut down their Asherim [goddesses]. You are not to bow in worship to any other god, for the Lord's name is Jealous. . . ."

The command to destroy is also in Deut. 7:16: "And you shall destroy all the

113

peoples that the Lord your God will give over to you, your eye shall not pity them; neither shall you serve their gods. . . ."

According to Deut. 13:12–16 whole pagan cities were to be destroyed.

There are many other texts in which the God of the Jews commanded the utter destruction of their compatriots simply because their blood brothers refused to fall in line. And blood brothers they were. For the Amorites, Hittites, and Canaanites were part-and-parcel of the same race as the Jews who had committed the genocide! Proof of this comes from the Old Testament itself. The prophet Ezekiel exclaims in 16:3: "Thus says the Lord God to Jerusalem: 'Your origin and your birth are in the land of the Canaanites; your father was an Amorite, and your mother was a Hittite.'"

Since Christianity is an outgrowth of Judaism, it follows that its intolerance, destruction, and genocide were inherited from its parent religion. Christianity justified its own heinous behavior by referring to the Jewish pasages as well as to its own texts. Matthew 27:25 says: "His [Christ's] blood be on us [the Jews who condemned Jesus] and on our children." John 8:44 tells us of the accusation by Jesus: "You [the Jews] are of your father the Devil. . . ."

The book of Revelation actually describes the great joy that will accompany vast destructions and killings. The "peacemaker" par excellence, Christ himself, is described as wearing a robe "dipped in blood" and as having a "mouth [from which] issues a sharp sword to smite the nations" (19:13–15).

Christian hatred reached out to many. Jesus said that if anyone did not hate his own family he could not be his disciple (Luke 14:26); that you are damned for not believing in him (Mark 16:16); and that anyone who "does not abide in me [Jesus], he is cast forth as a branch and withers; and the branches are gathered, thrown into the fire and burned " (John 15:6). In a parable Jesus approved of the slaying of his enemies (Luke 19:27).

Islam, whose God originates in Judaism and Christianity, is equally intolerant, destructive, and genocidal. Mohammed basically preached an utterly pure monotheism. Over and over again he insisted that there is no God but Allah.

At least half the Koran is taken up with denunciations of every form and suspicion of polytheism and idolatry.

Allah had no Son, no Wife, no Mother, no Holy Ghost. He was never to be represented in human form, by graven images, or in the trappings of sacraments. Mohammed did away with all human intermediaries between Allah and man, condemning priests and monks whom men have taken as Lords beside Allah. Denying the divinity of Christ, he insisted that he too was merely a man.

In spite of this, no higher religion is as despotic as Islam. While he remained as exclusive and jealous as the Jewish and Christians gods, granting salvation only to true believers, he was in fact even more arbitrary. He cursed the vast majority of men with unbelief, refusing to give any rational explanation for this psychotic scheme.

Nor did Allah allow anyone to question his moods nor, like Abraham who forced his God to accept human moral standards at Sodom and Gomorrah, did

Allah permit himself to be measured by human standards of justice. "The Lord of the Worlds is not under law," said a later theologian. This may very well be true but nevertheless is a regression to the barbarisms of earlier times. Allah insisted on the complete submission of men to his mysterious purposes. In fact, *Islam* means "complete surrender to the will of God," thus treating Allah with the universal prostration that the ancient men of the East had always displayed toward their kings and lords.

Mohammed legalized slavery, subordination of women, polygamy, eye-for-an-eye justice, and the "jihad"—the sacred duty to war upon idolaters. He commanded his followers to "slay the idolater wherever ye find him." Idol worshipers must either accept Islam, emigrate from the borders of Islam, or be put to death.

The Prophet preached a method of violence, not one of reasonable persuasion. He not only split mankind into righteous believers and sinners, he also denied human rights to unbelievers. His holy wars finally led to spiritual divisions in Islam.

Thus by its fruit shall you know the tree. Judaism and its two fanatical offspring, Christianity and Islam, demonstrate all too well the results of monotheism—intolerance, destruction, and genocide.

# 36

# Voltaire's Prayer

"My prayer to God is a short one: 'O Lord, make my enemies ridiculous.' God has granted it."

Voltaire's prayer has come true many times. What follows is simply one more.

Rabbi Isaac Leizerowski has a hobby, that of a scribe restoring Torah scrolls—holy parchments that consist of the five books of Moses. In an age in which writing has been replaced by word processing, some things that must still be done by hand. Jewish law says that this is one.

Writing a Torah scroll can take up to a year and costs at least $25,000. Once a scroll is written it must be maintained by certain standards. When it is beyond repair, it must be buried—like a dead human—in a Jewish cemetery.

To repair a scroll, certain ritual-like techniques must be used, for it is believed God has ordained it.

The parchment, known as *klaf,* must be made from the hide of a kosher animal, usually a cow or a sheep.

Black ink that is durable but not indelible is obligatory. It is cooked up from an old recipe: soot, oil, honey, vinegar, crushed gallnuts, gum Arabic, and metal powders. The Rabbi buys his ink ready-made in Jerusalem. He says he doesn't make it in his home because the stink would fill his house for weeks at a time.

And lettering must be done with a quill—one from a kosher bird!

The work is laborious. He might have to repair words or letters that have been cracked, worn away, or turned red with rust because of the iron oxides in the older inks. This calls for scraping the old ink off to expose a smooth surface that will hold new ink.

Erasing God's name is not allowed, so whenever he restores the name, he applies new ink over the old.

Rabbi Leizerowski says that the letters themselves have a "metaphysical aspect." He notes the mystical belief that every other Hebrew letter contains the form of a *yud* and a *vuv,* two single-stroke letters in the tetragrammaton, the four letters that stand for the name of God—*yud, hey, vuv, hey.* The rabbi continues: "There is a reasoning in each letter that maybe you don't know, but there is something godly in it. You can't be a scribe without realizing our incapacity to comprehend that."

He adds: "You cannot be an atheist and a scribe. You have the responsibility of making sure that the scroll is written according to all of the requirements that God has laid out for us."

The rabbi ought to realize that this kind of religious nonsense turns people to atheism.

Volatire's prayer has been answered many times—his enemies and ours have been made to look ridiculous.

# 37

# Why Jews Don't Eat Pork

In the Old Testament, Lev. 11:7-8 clearly proclaims that touching and eating the pig is off-limits. In other words, the boar or pig is taboo. This is how the text reads: ". . . the pig, because although it is a hoofed animal with cloven hoofs it does not chew the cud, and is unclean for you." This is reinforced by being repeated in Deut. 14:8.

A sacred animal was taboo and could not be eaten except in sacrifice to a special god. Like all taboos, on special occasions this prohibition was broken. According to the prophet Isaiah this taboo was set aside once a year at midwinter when there was a pig-feast, or the feast of the Boar's Head. Here's how the prophet rants against the practice: "Those who consecrate and purify themselves for garden-rites, one after the other in a magic ring, those who eat swine flesh, rats, and vile vermin will all meet their end, says the Lord" (Isa. 66:17).

Moreover, one of the names of the God of the Jews is Yahweh. This is usually translated into English as "the Lord." The Jews of later times stopped pronouncing the ineffable name of Yahweh and substituted for it the name Adonai, "Lord" (Isa. 1:24). My *American Heritage Dictionary* says that it comes from the Phoenician *adon* or "lord." And just two words down in the column is the word *Adonis*, also from the Phoenician "Adon." Just who was this "Adon/Adonis" and what's his connection with pigs?

Plutarch writes that the Greeks could not decide if the Jews worshiped swine or hated them. They were forbidden to eat the meat of a pig as well as not allowed to kill the animal. The rule against eating the pig indicates the animal was unclean (meaning sacred), and the law against killing them also shows that the pig was sacred. Since the Jews were in both Egypt and Syria, they assimilated the same attitude toward the pig.

The pig was considered a sacred animal in very early Egyptian history. It was regarded as the incarnation of the god Osiris, and thus was sanctified and endowed with supernatural powers. Thus, this is one place in which the Jews assimilated the holiness of the pig.

The Jews were also well involved with their neighbor Syria. In this territory Adonis (the lord) was a god of Byblos. He is described as a young hunter loved by Aphrodite (Astarte). He is killed in a chase by a wild boar, and bemoaned by his mistress. But long before this, the Lord Adonis was originally a sacred boar, worshiped by a clan of women who, in order to assimilate to their god, said they were sows. And once a year, a boar was killed, torn to pieces, and eaten at a communal feast—much as Isaiah says the Jews of his day did.

To us moderns this taboo seems strange and even ludicrous. And it is. Long ago the Jews had forgotten the origin and history of why they must not eat pork, much as Egyptian priests eventually forgot how to read their hieroglyphics.

Jewish authorities pretend that the biblical taboo on eating pig's flesh was a sensible precaution against trichinosis and other pig diseases. The fact is that the biblical authors knew nothing about the natural causes of disease and their Bible never associates any illness with the eating of unclean meats.

Insisting on such irrationalities as unclean meats being prohibited reminds me of the following question and answer:

Billy: "Why don't you go to our church?"

Sammy: " 'Cause we belong to a different abomination!"

# 38

# Pious Lies

NEWS HEADLINE: *Vatican Experts Lay Out Case Against Women As Priests.*
Follow-up: Marshaling its arguments to quash a debate that won't go away, the Vatican presented its most comprehensive case against women becoming Roman Catholic priests. The Church's long-standing argument, essentially, is that Christ was male and wanted his priests to be male, and the Church can't overrule that. The Church does not have the power to modify the practice, uninterrupted for two thousand years, of calling only men to the priesthood.

This is a prime example of a *pious lie*!

We know that the Church has modified its position on many important doctrines, incorporating pagan myths on one hand and ignoring biblical texts on the other. In this case the Church has ignored both the biblical charter for women priests as well as its own early history.

The New Testament and early Church Fathers give us telling evidence on women. The earliest evidence is from Paul's letters. Here women functioned as dynamic leaders of the movement (Phil. 4:2–3; Rom. 16), as deacons (Rom. 16:1–2), apostles (Rom. 16:7), and missionaries (1 Cor. 16:19; Rom. 16:3–4).

The Acts of the Apostles mention four daughters of Philip who *prophesied* (21:9), the *missionary* couple of Priscilla and Aquila (chapter 18), house-church *leaders* (12:12), and prominent converts (17:4, 12).

Thus, in pre-Pauline and Pauline Christian communities, women appear to have functioned *almost the same* as men. It may have been that more women than men were house-church leaders, hosting vital prayer meetings that became the kernel of the movement.

At least one woman *minister,* Phoebe, is recorded in Rom. 16:1–2. Here she functioned as an *official teacher and missionary* in the church of Cenchreae. Euodia and Syntyche from Philippi were prominent *leaders* of the community (Phil. 4:2–3).

Junia served the church as an *apostle* as we learn in Rom. 16:7.

The most prominent woman in the New Testament is Priscilla, who worked alongside her husband and may have been the more renowned of the pair (1 Cor. 16:19; Rom. 16:3–4; Acts 18).

The women named Mary, Tryphaena, Tryphosa, and Persis in Romans 16 are described having labored for the Lord, the *same term* Paul used to describe his own evangelizing and teaching activities.

Despite attempts by the hierarchy through the centuries to conceal the evidence, there are written recordings of women priests into the Byzantine era. An epistle of Pope Gelasius (492–96) to bishops in Italy and Sicily mentions in annoyance that women were officiating at sacred altars and taking part in ecclesiastical affairs supposedly handled only by men.

This is buttressed by an inscription from Brutium dated to the end of the fifth century that mentions the presbytera Leta, and another from Salona in Dalmatia (425) tells us of the prebytera Flavia Vitalia.

All of this verifies that women for at least a quarter of the life of the Roman Catholic Church performed the same functions as male priests and that male bishops ordained them. This is merely one more illustration of the pious lies the Church has tried to perpetuate.

# 39

# Have the Fundamentalists Got It Wrong!

Yes, Protestant Fundamentalists have it wrong, all wrong when they say that because the Bible is sacred it follows that the text is self-revealing and unalterable, that interpretation is not needed, and indeed, if done verges on blasphemy. Any study of the attitudes and religious activities of the very people who put the Bible together would show how very wrong Fundamentalists are.

Did the Jews take their Bible literally? Not at all! How do we know? Why, any study of how Jews interpret and reinterpret the Torah—the first five books of Moses—will show great flexibility, and even greater contradictions, in their response to the biblical text.

The Torah was canonically established by Ezra and Nehemiah in the fifth century before Christ. You can read about this in the Jewish Bible. This just about sealed the text against change. So the Jews initiated the custom of having an interpreter present in the synagogue to explain complex passages whenever the Torah was read aloud. Since it became more and more difficult to interpret ancient injunctions so they seemed relevant to contemporary problems, the interpreters began to stray from the text, offering more pertinent or imaginary interpretations. Thus was born exegesis, a so-called science of analysis and interpretation called Midrash ("exposition"). In time this became part of the Talmud.

Then out of the Midrash came the Mishnah ("repetition"), a more advanced commentary and interpretation. The Mishnah apparently was developed independently in the two centers of Judaism at the time, Palestine and Babylonia. The Pharisees (party of the common people led by rabbis) held Mishnah to be an exalted effort to probe for God's meaning. This was opposed by the Sadducees, who held to a literalist position—much as the Protestant Fundamentalists do today.

The masses took to the Mishnah with great enthusiasm. Now the ordinary Jew could read the holy books and discuss and question the sages' interpretations. New exegetes rose from the common people—their occupations were no longer a bar to the once-priestly privilege and monopoly of interpreting the holy books. Since the rabbis feared that the Mishnah would grow and thereby supplant the Torah, they decreed that no one could write down any Mishnah. This meant that the Mishnah had to be memorized and could be passed on only orally. Hence, Mishnah became known as the "oral law."

A great first century (C.E.) debate waged between the sages Hillel and Shammai and their ardent disciples. Shammai was a conservative, strict textual follower and a legalist. Hillel was a "liberal," a philosopher-humanist. Today, Shammai would be called a "strict Constitutionalist," Hillel a "loose Constitutionalist." He was less concerned with property rights than human rights. Hillel's views finally won out.

Akiba, who died around 135 C.E., was the greatest scholar of his time. Thousands of students flocked to him. He perfected his own method of biblical exegesis, and collected the oral law which he classified by subject matter. His great work was used by Judah Ha-Nasi and his coworkers as the basis of a written Mishnah.

Judah Ha-Nasi ("the Prince," about 135-200 C.E.), a great scholar, feared that the Mishnah would depart too far from the Torah, thereby creating heresies, so he declared the Mishnah closed. Now the "oral law" was frozen.

But such fundamental constraints succeeded no more in Judaism than in any other religion. In the yeshivas (Jewish schools) of Babylonia there soon arose, primarily from several of Judah Ha-Nasi's disciples, a continuation of Torah interpretation. This is called the Gemara ("supplement"). This Gemara observed the restrictions governing the oral law, used Aramaic instead of Hebrew as its language and, at first, appeared to be simply an extension of the Mishnah itself. Like Midrash, like Mishnah, so Gemara was strictly oral for centuries, and the academies in Babylonia reigned as authority in Judaic thought and discussion from 200 to 600 C.E. This was put into written form in the sixth century C.E. because of several severe pogroms against the Jews (and Christians too) in Persia who were very much afraid that all this would be lost.

As you can see, there was a constant need for the Jews to update their religion or ossify into an archaic culture. The Talmud is very much available today and anyone may read and study it. It embraces everything from theology to contracts, cosmology to cosmetics, jurisprudence to etiquette, criminal law to diet, delusions, and drinking. It roams from exegesis to esthetics. It is crammed with anecdotes, aphorisms, thumbnail biographies, and philosophical treatises, as well as tiresome hair-splitting arguments. It is majestic and pedantic, brilliant and dreary, insightful and trivial, awesome and obscure, superstitious and casuistic. Sophistry runs amuck, abracadabras abound, and profundity often ends in mythology, astrology, and numerology. Like Catholic scholastics, the Talmudists spent a lot of time and effort in an intellectual no-man's land.

The Talmud is not dogma. It is not a catechism. It illustrates the ways in which biblical passages can be interpreted, argued over, and reinterpreted. Over its many pages, arguments rage and views clash.

The Talmud is a vast collection of sixty-three books. For our purposes, it must be emphasized that here are learned debates, heated arguments, dialogues, conclusions, commentaries, commentaries upon commentaries, and commentaries upon commentaries upon commentaries of the scholars who interpreted the Torah over a thousand years and constantly updated its views on problems of law, ethics, ceremony, and traditions. In view of this, It's impossible to believe that millions of Protestant Fundamentalists are still blind to the fact that the very people who originated and live by the Bible find it necessary to constantly reinterpret their sacred texts. They should get a revelation, either from their God or from the Jews or from us secular humanists, that it is irrational to interpret the Bible literally.

# 40

# A "Dear John" Letter to Creationists

Let me present an imaginary scenario. *If* I had once sided with creationists and finally saw the light, I would have had to write a "Dear John" letter, insisting that I am now abandoning their bizarre, unscientific explanations.

I would have pointed out that Irish Archbishop James Ussher in 1650 figured the Earth's age at six thousand years as way, way too young. I bought his arithmetic that consisted of counting the biblical accounts of generations begetting other generations. I felt that in his time there wasn't very much else other than the Bible to go on. But what I can't understand today is the stubbornness of my former colleagues who still accept Ussher's error. After all, even back in the 1700s, long before Darwin, people did see contrary evidence of an older Earth in rock formations and fossil records.

My enlightenment saw how ridiculous it was to hold onto the clerical coat-tails of the good bishop. Mainstream science convinced me to give up the creationist ghost. Science now places the age of Earth's oldest rocks at around four billion years, based on scientific instruments which measure the decay of radioactive elements within them. Similar dating techniques probing moon rocks and meteorites place the age of the Earth at 4.6 billion years.

As a former creationist I used to argue that fossils, including the skeletons of dinosaurs, came from animals that lived no longer than six thousand years ago. And those animals that no longer exist died in the great flood of Noah's time. When I was asked about the layers of sediment that appear to have built up over millions of years, I would hand out a video about the eruption of Mount St. Helens in 1980. This tape argued that the hundreds of layers of volcanic ash were built up within hours of the eruption. This supposedly proved that large geologic formations can build up quickly and catastrophically. But what I did not disclose about the tape was that scientists can actually tell the difference between layers of sediment deposited by water and layers of volcanic ash—so the video was lying, a sin I hope is forgiven with this mea culpa.

I now also realize that all kinds of processes would have had to happen ridiculously fast in order to have a young Earth. For instance, the Grand Canyon would have to have been carved out in just days, and the mile-thick limestone deposits found nearby would have to have grown at the rate of twenty-five inches a day!

My former creationists also have a big problem with astrophysicists. For they have shown that many stars and galaxies are millions, and even billions of light-years away, meaning that their light has taken that many years to reach us.

Creationists also have a lot of trouble with one of Einstein's findings— namely, that the speed of light is constant. We used to say Einstein was wrong because the Lord is powerful enough to change the speed of light if he wants to.

I must confess that I found finally that all the creationists do is to mix up more or less science with more or less scripture, producing results that are more or less absurd.

Well, thank God that is all behind me. I only hope that it does not take my former creationist buddies light-years to catch up with the scientific findings that compelled me to change my mind.

# 41

# The Theological Sins of the Creationists

Great are the sins of the creationists, for they have doubly damned themselves by perverting both science and religion. A memorable job of refutation has been done on them concerning their aberrations regarding science. The time has come to do the same concerning their misreading of their Bibles.

Before doing so, two of their basic assumptions must be reviewed. Creationists claim that the Bible is the inspired Word of God, quoting from Heb. 11:3: "By faith we understand that the world was created by the word of God."

To make their idea about the inspiration of the Bible quite clear, let me quote from an interview with Jerry Falwell in *Penthouse* magazine.

> *Penthouse*: Do you believe the sort of things [found in the Bible] like Lot's wife being turned into a pillar of salt?
>
> Falwell: I do.
>
> *Penthouse*: Do you also believe the Bible when it says that serpents spoke and things like that?
>
> Falwell: Oh, of course. Absolutely. And so would over half the preachers in America. . . . That is what the Christian church was built upon, and it's only when we've gotten away from it that we've gotten in trouble.

These Protestant Fundamentalists, as led by Falwell and others, have a concept of the inspiration of the Bible that fortifies the creationists. This attitude gives them the greatest confidence to accept the origin of the universe and all of life as described in Genesis as true.

One author on creationism says boldly in his textbook: "This course is designed to show the student that the Bible is dependable and that those proposed theories that conflict with scripture have no valid basis."

To see if these assumptions hold water, let's first explore the biblical text

127

itself. The typical passage used to "prove" that God created "ex nihilo"—out of nothing—is Gen. 1:1: "In the beginning God created the heaven and the earth." This would seem to fit their argument of creation out of nothing. Yet, modern translations, either directly or in a footnote disagree, saying: "When God began to create. . . ." This is an entirely different idea, for it means that before God began to create there was already present chaotic material substances out of which God created order. The cosmos was already there; all God's "Wind" or "Spirit" did was to create order out of chaos.

The reason modern translators changed the passage is that long after the King James version was done, scholars discovered that all the ancients, Jews included, thought that the creative acts of deity were to bring order out of the aboriginal chaotic materials the deity found at hand. How the disordered cosmos got there in the first place did not enter their speculations.

The "Wind" or "Spirit" of God is taken by the creationists to be the Holy Ghost, the third member of the Trinity and referred to frequently in the New Testament. But no New Testament author says that the Holy Ghost was present at the creation.

The text of Genesis clearly states that it was God alone that did the creating. This is accepted by the creationists. Yet, there is a contradiction in their argument, because Paul and the authors of the Fourth Gospel and Hebrews declare that Jesus existed in some form before his incarnation and therefore took part in the creation.

Paul states this equal sharing in the act of creation to the Father *and* Son in 1 Cor. 8:6: "Yet for us there is one God, the Father, and one Lord, Jesus Christ, through whom are all things, and we exist for him. . . ." Then in Col. 1:15–16, Paul names the Son as the Creator, eliminating the Father altogether!

Moving to the Fourth Gospel, the author (supposedly John) says in his Prologue that the "Word" became flesh and existed "at the beginning" and made all things (John 1:2–3). Although Jesus Christ was with God from the beginning, it was through the Son that creation came about. Like Paul, John too cuts out the role of the Father in creation.

Switching to Heb. 1:10–12, the writer quotes Ps. 102:25–27, inserting the word "Lord"—one of Jesus' titles—and ascribes to him the creation of the heavens and the Earth.

Thus we see that on the basis of these biblical passages the creationists have grievously sinned. They have violated their own principle of "divine inspiration," for anyone can now see that their so-called inspired text is contradictory. Just who was the Creator, God alone, or his Son, or both? I don't see how the creationists can worm their way out of this!

There are more coals to heap on the creationists. The Bible does not confine God's activity to only the original creation as described in Genesis. It depicts activities in which God is continuously creating! According to Col. 1:17 the Son continues to "hold all things together." God turns each night into day and each day into night (Amos 5:8). He makes the sea rage and then calms the storm again

(Ps. 107:25–29). All that God does for the rest of creation is matched by what he continuously does for man. He keeps him alive (Ps. 66:8 f.) and continuously provides for him (145:15 f.).

Even Jesus, Savior and God to the creationists, clearly states that creation is continuous. When Jesus is accused by the Jews of breaking the law by healing a cripple on the sabbath, he justified his action by referring to his Father's work of sustaining the universe which must go on continuously if life is to be maintained: "My Father is working still . . ." (John 5:17).

In spite of all this activity, God never tires: "He does not faint or grow weary" (Isa. 40:28).

Creationists, therefore, are completely wrong in both their assumptions and their conclusions. They have sinned grievously against their God and their Lord Jesus—for they have perverted the meaning of Holy Writ to satisfy their own selfish motives. The greatest sin of all, however, is their sin against truth!

# 42

# Revelations about the Apocalypse and the Fundamentalists

Christian Fundamentalists put great store in the prophecies of the book of Revelation. They claim that its predictions are actually coming true today. Are they fooling themselves as well as conning the rest of us?

Revelation is the last tract in the New Testament. The Greek title of the book is the "Apocalypse of John." The word apocalypse is a transliteration of the Greek word for "revelation." Any writing under this title claims to include a revelation of hidden things imparted by God, especially a revelation of events hidden in the future.

To understand this difficult book, you need to know something about Jewish Christianity, its primitive church in Jerusalem, and about the Roman Emperor Nero. You will have to appreciate that its author, St. John the Divine, was a Christian prophet, having visions because the Spirit of God inspired him to move to heights of ecstasy.

The basic theme of the Apocalypse is that the Parthians, an eastern people who controlled the old Persian empire, will soon dominate the world under the leadership of a resurrected Nero. Although the Parthians would bring about the downfall of Rome, the final and decisive victory would be Israel's.

This story cannot be found in any apocalypse before that of John. It is an elaborate folktale about the second coming of Nero from Parthia. (Such a coming reminds us of Christ's second coming, as we shall see later.) The question now is: what has Nero to do with Parthia?

Ever since Augustus had allowed himself to be worshiped as a god, each of his successors was also considered a god.

The Emperor Nero (C.E. 54–68) was immediately hailed by the poet Calpurnius Siculus as a god as soon as he ascended the throne. The poet tells us that at this moment a comet blazed a trail in the sky for twenty straight nights because Nero was a prince of peace as well as a savior who would return the earth to its original state of paradise. No wonder this same motif was applied to Jesus who was thought by his followers to be King of Kings, certainly king of the Jews according to Mark 15:18. Apparently, much of the known world was vibrating with this powerful myth.

After Nero had run himself through with a sword along his collarbone and bled to death, there were still people who believed that the young Emperor was still alive and would return to wreak vengeance on his enemies. Suetonius, a Roman historian of the second century, tells us that Nero was very popular among the Parthians. The reason for this is that Nero sent his best general, Corbulo, to restore Armenia to the Parthians, who had lost it to a usurper. The new Armenian ruler, Tiridates, brother of the Parthian king Volgaeses, agreed to accept the crown of Armenia from the hands of Nero. He traveled to Rome in regal style and accepted his investiture at Rome with great splendor.

So popular was Nero with the Parthians that during the time in which the Apocalypse was written an unknown imposter did indeed pretend to be Nero. He received so much Parthian support that it was only after long and hesitant deliberations that he was finally extradited and handed over to the Romans. This is how the tale of Nero Redivivus originated. It continued with the emperor rising from the dead, escaping to Parthia and then returning again to Italy at the head of Parthian troops to wreak vengeance on his enemies and to destroy Rome.

The Jews also took over this legend, as can be seen in the fifth book of the Sibylline Oracles. These were actually composed by all sorts of people from the beginning of the Christian era, including both Jews and Jewish Christians. A passage from the fifth book says: "But he, the baneful one [Nero] will disappear without a trace and will afterward return, making himself equal with God; but He shall unmask him and show that he is not God."

This matches exactly with the beast who John says: ". . . was and now is not but will come again" (Rev. 17:8). For the beast of the Apocalypse is none other than Nero!

The Sibylline Oracles also disclose another prediction which was used advantageously by their Jewish and Jewish Christian composers: "The treasures received by Rome from Asia, its tributary, shall be restored to Asia by Rome threefold, and every injury shall be avenged upon her; all Asiatic slaves who served in Italian houses, twenty times as many Italians shall serve as slaves in Asia and in poverty, and they shall pay off debts that cannot be numbered."

Thus the transformation of a pagan folktale by Jewish Christians is an important key to unlocking the meaning of the Apocalypse. Both Jewish Christianity and the book are rooted in the actual historical period in which it was written. At the same time, the book is both eternal and inimitable, for it has reached far beyond the confines of the Christian congregation which John originally intended to console with its message.

Throughout every era that followed, including our own computer age, it has inspired artists and rebels alike, pious women and devout men, fanatics as well as the lunatic fringe. No other document has managed to articulate so urgently the idea that our world is facing a catastrophe—or to conjure up such a convincing picture of the glorious future which awaits mankind after the last, decisive conflict. This is still true today; you have only to read the literature or to listen to the ravings of Fundamentalist preachers.

To see that these Fundamentalists either have no idea of the actual reason why the Apocalypse was written—or are engaging in a gigantic, unconscionable hoax on their duped followers—you merely have to read a book by one of their spokesmen, Hal Lindsey's *The Late Great Planet Earth.* In the gospel according to Lindsey, the prophets foresaw the future and spelled it out with remarkable accuracy. As we near the end of history, says Lindsey, certain national powers will appear as signs of the end and the coming of Jesus Christ. The Common Market will be formed in the new Rome; Russia will rise militarily; the United States will become a Christian nation and the light of the world. Most important of all, though, is the modern triumph of Israel, Judaism, and the Jews. Why?

Because Israel is all-important as the staging ground for the return of Jesus and the beginning of the millennium. The only good Jew will be a Christianized Jew—hence the rise of Messianic Jewish cults to convert Jews to Christianity. We can do no better to combat this cosmic absurdity than by understanding the historical background of the Apocalypse and by laughing again with H. L. Mencken's description of the Scopes trial which, in his day, had become a contest between Fundamentalism and modernity.

Mencken summed up the scene as "an obscenity of the very first calibre." He then fleshed out his generalization: "There was a friar wearing a sandwich board announcing that he was the Bible champion of the world. There was a Seventh Day Adventist arguing that Clarence Darrow was the beast with seven heads and ten horns described in Revelation 13, and that the end of the world was at hand. There was an evangelist made up like Andy Gump [a comic strip character] with the news that atheists in Cincinnati were preparing to descend upon Dayton, hang the eminent Judge Ralston, and burn the town. There was the ancient who maintained that no Catholic could be a Christian. There was the eloquent Dr. T. T. Martin of Blue Mountain, Mississippi, come to town with a truckload of torches and hymnbooks to put Darwin in his place. There was a singing brother bellowing apocalyptic hymns. . . . Dayton was having a roaring time."

And so should we as we evaluate the book of Revelation.

# SCIENCE VERSUS RELIGION

# 43

# Monkeyshines at the Monkey Trial

In 1925 the attention of the United States and western Europe focused on the yawning little town of Dayton, Tennessee. It was here that the Fundamentalists dug in their heels, determined to win the battle of Armageddon. They were on the side of God's creation as described in the book of Genesis and against the evolutionary ideas of the Antichrist.

Because he had violated the state's law forbidding the teaching of evolution in the public schools, teacher John T. Scopes was brought to trial. Clarence Darrow, one of the foremost lawyers of the country, came to his rescue. Just as quickly, William Jennings Bryan, three times a losing candidate for the presidency of the United States and a born Fundamentalist, chose to join forces with the prosecution.

Throughout the trial, vilification and blatant ignorance was a common practice on both sides. This was to be expected in a social context in which the encrusted past was making a "Custer's last stand" against a youthful, cocksure science. A. T. Stewart, chief lawyer of the prosecution, referred to Darrow as "the greatest menace present-day civilization has to deal with."

Judge Ben G. McKenzie, a leader of the Dayton bar, did not preside at the trail, but offered the judgment that Darrow and the men around him "had better go back to their homes, the seat of thugs, thieves and haymarket rioters and educate their criminals, than try to proselyte here in the South."

The little-known author of the Tennessee anti-evolution law was "honest" John Butler. His preacher had made a very fine sermon one Sunday, telling how bad this evolution was, and how it was contrary to the book of Genesis, and how it was being taught in high school and likely to turn our young people into infidels.

Having three boys of his own, Butler sat down the next day at his own kitchen table and wrote out the best he could a bill against letting this evolution be taught in the schools. The next morning he took his rough draft to the legislature at the capital where he was a senator and had the secretary of state, who was good at legal language, put the bill in the right words. Then Senator Butler introduced his bill and saw it passed.

Later during the trial, the judge refused to let the defense lawyers introduce expert scientists to tell what evolution was, causing John Butler to become the most indignant person in the courtroom. He was heard to say: "That ain't fair. He ought to give 'em a chance to tell what it is. 'Course we have 'em licked anyhow, but I believe in bein' a fair 'n square American at all times. Besides, I'd like to know what evolution is myself!" This from the man who wrote the bill!

H. L. Mencken was on hand as a reporter. At the close of the first day's proceedings, he gave a summary in just two eloquent words: "Damnable obscenity!"

Anyone looking for a cynical, caustic columnist would select him last in a crowd, for his face was saintlike. His eyes were innocent, light buttercup blue; his complexion peaches and cream; and his brown hair was parted geometrically down the middle. He looked so sweet that every woman wanted to chuck him under the chin and to talk baby talk to him. But this never stopped Mencken from firing his cannons. Here's how he vilified the area: "Tennessee needs only fifteen minutes of free speech to become civilized."

But the words which caused the greatest excitement were exchanged by the champions of the past and present in the climactic final days. Bryan had himself sworn in as a witness for the prosecution, and when Darrow, the agnostic enemy, rose to cross-examine, Armageddon was joined.

Darrow led Bryan through a detailed tour of Genesis. "Yes," agreed Bryan, "the serpent had been punished by God because it had tempted Eve."

And then . . .

Darrow: Do you think that is why the serpent is compelled to crawl upon its belly?

Bryan: I believe that.

Darrow: Have you any idea how the snake went before that time?

Bryan: No sir.

Darrow: Do you know whether he walked on his tail or not?

Malicious laughter crackled throughout the hot, sweaty courtroom. Bryan jumped from his chair, stretched his arms out to the howling audience, and shouted an appeal to his followers: "I want the world to know that this man, who does not believe in God, is trying to use the Tennessee court to slur at it. . . ."

Darrow broke in: "I object to your statement. I am examining you on your fool ideas that no intelligent Christian on earth believes."

Just before Scopes was fined one hundred dollars, everyone made little speeches, exchanging flattery all around, except that Darrow said in his usual devastating way, "I think this case will be remembered because it is the first case of this sort since we stopped trying people in America for witchcraft, because here we have done our best to turn back the tide that has sought to force itself upon this modern world—of testing every fact in science by a religious dictum."

After the trial was over, one of the observers who was about to step onto the departing train asked Scopes, "Johnny, I'd like to ask you a question before I leave. Did you ever really teach evolution in the Rhea County High School?"

Scopes answered with a broad grin: "In the high school I'm a science teacher, or at least I was. Taught chemistry and biology and such. But my hardest job was coach in athletics—football in the fall, basketball in the spring. I was pretty busy. Sometimes we had to use the biology period for planning our plays, and I reckon likely we never did get around to that old evolution lesson. But the kids were good sports and wouldn't squeal on me in court!"

A few weeks after the trial, Bryan died in Tennessee after a day of much speech making. Writing his obituary for the *Baltimore Sun,* Mencken began with a vicious question:

"Has it been duly marked by historians that William Jennings Bryan's last secular act on this globe of sin was to catch flies?"

# 44

# The War between Science and Religion

Stephen Hawking, hailed as probably the most brilliant theoretical physicist since Einstein, and his good friend and companion physicist Bernard Carr, went to Rome in 1975, where the Vatican awarded its Pius II medal to Hawking for distinguished work by a young scientist. Carr says that Hawking had a great affinity with Galileo, which touched off Carr's thoughts about the controversy between the Catholic Church and Galileo. In turn, this triggered Carr's comment that "the controversy between science and religion still rages."

In contrast, there are groups today which believe that science and religion are merely two sides of the coin of human experience and therefore have much in common. Such was the feeling of Andrew D. White, one of the cofounders of Cornell University and author of the classic *A History of the Warfare of Science with Theology in Christendom*. Note that White judges the conflict is between science and theology, not science and religion.

However, noted American historian and scientist John W. Draper disagreed. He wrote the classic *The Conflict Between Religion and Science*. Note this time that the argument has shifted from science's war with theology to its war with religion.

To see who's right, let's put them under a microscope . . .

Religion fervently believes, and even shouts its faith, Kierkegaard-like, refusing to go all the way in its questioning. When Hawking went again to a conference at the Vatican in 1981, he had an audience with Pope John Paul II. Said Hawking: "He told us that it was all right to study the evolution of the universe after the big bang, but we should not inquire into the big bang itself because that was the moment of creation and therefore the work of God."

In contrast, science depends on skepticism for its mother's milk, using this nourishment to energize its continuing search for answers no matter where it leads.

Religion wraps itself in the security blanket of the settled and the final, always yearning for the first sacred revelations when God and man were friends in an idyllic Garden of Eden. Thus religion handcuffs itself to the sacred past. Not science. It unlocks these shackles, freeing us to pursue a secular future. Religion looks backward to a Golden Age and imagines an unworldly future of heaven and hell. Science looks to the world of here and now, insisting that religion's heaven and hell is what man makes of his life in this world.

Science constantly exercises its curiosity. Like a quarterback, it insists on thrusting forward, and if it can, making touchdown after touchdown. Like football, science is open-ended in that there is no limit to the amount it can score. Its achievements are limitless, limited only to the skills of its players and the validity of its playbook.

Religion has been whistling in the graveyard, like a priest repeating magic formulas and swinging incense to keep menacing ghosts away. Science has advanced boldly—many times fighting the priest and his church—exorcising these ghosts with reality by writing equations and fingering its microscopes and telescopes.

Religion insists it has the truth, that it has knowledge once and for all of the Unknown. Science admits its partial ignorance and its contingency. The gnosis of religion concerns the unprovable; that of science of what is provable by mathematics and experiment.

Religion knows gods, goddesses, devils, angels, things that "go bump in the night"; science only fallible men.

Religion is a form of psychic anthropomorphism, where man is made in the image of the Unknown, an imaginative entity supposedly alive, personal, omnipotent, omnipresent. Science tries manfully to rid itself of such subjective human and superman characteristics. Religion seeks some inscrutable Person, some Platonic Noble Lie to submit to. Science strives for an understanding and domination of reality, even trying to make the irrational rational. The shaman of the sanctuary has been replaced by the scientist in the lab.

Religion is wishful thinking, emotionally based, Milquetoast-tenderminded, Dioynsian. Science throws away the magician's wand of illusion, being objectively oriented, John Wayne-toughminded, Apollonian.

Religion derives ultimately from someone's mystic, moonlighting state, one that is beyond any human comprehension, one which cannot be described with the precision of equations and formulas, and one which has no language except the inadequate one of metaphor. If it must, science creates new languages so that anyone who wants to can participate and understand.

Religion tends to the me-tooism of the cult, fostering ill will and even mayhem to outsiders. Paradoxically, it also encourages individualism where belief is as private as one's bowel movements. Science is public, goldfish-bowlish, international. Each individual's offering is meticulously examined under the microscope, through the telescope, and in the atom smasher.

Religion supposes values came once and for all from Mount Sinai, that they were written in the permanence of stone and in the consciences of men by the hand of God. Science realizes that all there is and all there will be is man, that he must and does make values by and for himself.

Religious ritual tends to forget its original meaning, often masking this memory loss by adding new perfume to the old stink, and theology all too often forgets what it is talking about. Voltaire put it well when he said that theology was "a science profound, supernatural, and divine, which teaches us to reason on that which we don't understand and to get our ideas mixed up on that which we do."

Science realizes full well that its symbols are merely tools extending man's limited senses, thereby revealing the unsuspected animalcules under the microscope of a Leeuwenhoek. When the language no longer fits, science rubbishes it, replacing it with a new slang that is arresting, concrete, and precise.

Religion in order to hold onto its old beliefs becomes ever more sophistical, practicing infanticide upon the progeny of the ancients, attempting the art of proving anything and therefore the habit of believing everything. Science discards the inadequate baggage of a portmanteau for better luggage which helps in traveling to the future.

Those who find no war between our sacred and secular culture not only have no sense of what happened in history but also have no insight into the meaning, nature, and purpose of their beliefs, or the grounds on which they are held.

Each dead society has bequeathed us its sickness: the Greeks with their Platonism as the Great Tradition in Western philosophy; the Jews with their fallen temple of ancient tribalisms and their lost Davidic messiah in the guise of Jesus the Christ; and the Romans with their ghost of autocracy haunting us in the arrogant pretense of the Church's political and intellectual despotism.

Today, science and its coworker technology now understand the perils of fossil folkways. Science should educate all mankind in this atomic age—if we will only let it.

Poll after poll shows with great irony that in the most scientifically and technologically oriented country in the world today, Americans by and large are scientific pygmies.

Could it be that no life has been found on other planets because long ago in their wars between science and religion, religion had won?

# 45

# The Devil, Science!

In both the Old and New Testaments we find magic, witchcraft, and soothsaying referred to as real. In contrast to these archaic ideas, we see that much more rational ideas came from the nature philosophers of Greece. Their intellectual curiosity began by claiming that both nature and human experience may be explained by pure reason rather than by supernatural causes. Thus, the earliest Greek philosophy was based on natural science. Representatives of these free-thinkers were Thales, Anaximander, and Anaximenes.

These natural philosophers must not be confused with the views held by either Plato or Aristotle. Plato had developed a world in which the physical sciences had little if any real reason for existing. And Aristotle conceived of a world in which the same sciences, although developed largely by observation of what is, was even more interested in speculation of what *ought* to be.

When Christianity was established, and with it a marked emphasis on theology, the normal development of science was choked off for over fifteen hundred years.

Why? Because the now powerful Church created an atmosphere in which science could hardly grow—a poisoned environment for those sniffing at Nature to find its truths. There was the general belief carried over from the New Testament that the end of the world was at hand, that the last judgment was approaching, and that the physical world was soon to be destroyed. For these reasons the greatest thinkers of the Church poured contempt upon all natural philosophers, insisting that everything except the saving of souls was useless, and that the worldly sciences were "absurdities" and "fooleries."

Then there was the established standard to which all struggling science had to conform—a standard which favored magic rather than science, a standard of rigid dogmatism gotten from the literal reading of the Bible.

But after a thousand years, the end of all things seemed further off than ever, taking the theological starch out of the churchmen. This and other reasons forced the twelth and thirteenth centuries to come out of this intellectual cocoon. Along with the cathedral builders and Thomas Aquinas came a new spirit of inquiry, led by Albert the Great and Roger Bacon, both of whom instituted the experimental method. Unlucky for us and science, Aquinas was most persuasive in elevating theology over science, making theology the "Queen of Sciences." How wrong he was! In Aquinas's commentary on Aristotle's *Heaven and Earth,* he gave us a striking example of the nonsense that occurs when theological reasoning and the literal interpretation of the Bible are mixed with scientific facts.

Another factor used to combat science was the idea that science was *dangerous*—an attitude still with some of us. This belief was very old, presumably beginning when Egyptian magicians made great demands which, if not fulfilled, led to threats that they would reach out to the four corners of the earth, pull down the pillars of heaven, and wreck the living places of the gods above and crush those of the men below.

Under Christianity such pagan threats were replaced, this time by the active interference of Satan in magic. The myth of Satan had come into Judaism when the Jews were in Persian captivity, then passed into Christianity with a vengeance. Church theologians stressed such prooftexts as that of the Psalmist, who said that "all the gods of the heathen are devils," and of Paul, who wrote that "the things which the Gentiles sacrifice, they sacrifice to devils." It was widely held that these devils were naturally indignant at being displaced and therefore anxious to revenge themselves upon Christians. Magicians were held to be agents of these dethroned gods, and this was further reinforced by those who practiced magic because these imposters pretended to have supernatural powers, using rites and phrases inherited from paganism.

So as soon as Christianity became the state religion, Emperor Constantine after his conversion enacted the severest of laws against magicians and magic in which the practitioner could be burnt alive. And each of his succeeding emperors increased the pressure against all kinds of magic. By the twelth and thirteenth centuries the terror of magic and witchcraft took complete possession of the people. It infused sculpture, painting, and literature, as well as the lives of the saints.

All of the Church's greatest theologians accepted and spread this belief. It was argued that, as the Devil afflicted Job, so he and his minions continued to cause diseases. It was contended that, as Satan was the prince of the power of the air, he and his followers caused storms. It was held that the cases of Nebuchadnezzar and Lot's wife who was changed into a pillar of salt proved that sorcerers could transform human beings into animals and even lifeless matter. It was believed that, as the devils of Gadara were cast into swine by Jesus, all animals could be afflicted in the same way. It was accepted that, as Christ himself had been transported through the air by the power of Satan, so any person could be transported to any high mountain.

The horror of magic and witchcraft kept increasing. By 1317 Pope John XXII issued a bull leveled at the alchemists, with the result that not only were the charlatans caught in the net but all other practitioners, dealing the beginnings of chemistry a terrible blow. Pope John, by virtue of his infallibility as the world's teacher in matters of faith and morals, condemned both real science and pseudoscience. To get the flavor of this great irrationality, listen to Pope John. He complains in two of his documents that both he and his flock are in danger of their lives from sorcerers, that such sorcerers can send devils into mirrors and finger rings, can kill men and women by a magic word, and that they had tried to kill him by sticking a wax figure of him with needles in the name of the Devil. He therefore called on all ecclesiastical and secular rulers to hunt down these criminals, especially increasing the powers of inquisitors throughout Europe. This attitude against the investigation of nature was felt for centuries so that chemistry came to known as one of the "seven devilish arts."

The Protestant Reformation did not change this antiscientific attitude. From Augustine to Thomas Aquinas, from Aquinas to Luther, and from Luther to Wesley, theologians from both branches of Christianity promoted the belief in magic and witchcraft. In this atmosphere scientific investigators had to practically run for their lives or go into hiding. The charge that science was in league with Satan was overwhelming. Pope Alexander put this most forcefully in one of his bulls, saying that studying physics or the laws of this world "shall be avoided by all and excommunicated."

Since then we've come a long way. Scientists rightfully are no longer thought to be in league with the Devil. Back in the thirteenth century Roger Bacon put science on the right path. He said the sciences must rest on mathematics, stating neatly that mathematics is "the alphabet of philosophy." Speculative argument is never enough to establish a conclusion; direct inspection is necessary. Thus experimental science is superior to speculative science. Bacon then summarized: "There are two modes of acquiring knowledge, namely by reasoning and experience. Reasoning draws a conclusion and makes us grant the conclusion, but does not make the conclusion certain, nor does it remove doubt so that the mind may rest on the intuition of truth, unless the mind discovers it by the path of experience."

# 46

# Islam and Science

Physicist Freeman Dyson, in an article about the how Western science grew out of Christian theology, recently paraphrased Nobel Prize-winning Muslim physicist Abdus Salam. He wrote that Salam had happily proclaimed his Muslim faith and at the same time that Salam felt no conflict between his faith and science.

It is the height of irony that the same Salam who benefited from the fruits of Western scientific knowledge should purposely have ignored the advances made by that same West in its exploration of Muslim scriptures and theology.

Is the Muslim laureate right? Is there no conflict between his religion and science?

How could Salam, as well as the bulk of other Muslims, ignore the findings, implications, and insights of such Western scholars as Bauer, Strauss, Wrede, Renan, Feuerbach, Nietzsche, Freud, Wells, and a host of others? Hume's rebuttal of miracles is equally valid in the Islamic context—for even Muslims attest to the miracles of Jesus! The Koran contains references to many Old and New Testament figures: Enoch, Noah, Abraham, Ishmael, Isaac, Jacob, Moses, David, Jonah, and Jesus, to name but a few.

The rise of critical methods developed in nineteenth-century Germany spread elsewhere. With its application to the study of the Bible and religion in general have come certain devastating conclusions that must be taken into account. When Western biblical scholars say that Samson was a merely a legend, that Jonah never existed, and that Moses did not write the Pentateuch, then, by implication, the truth of the Koran is also called into question.

Such an analytical searchlight has, of course, been turned on both the Koran and the Muslim religion. So it is not a question that such criticism has not been applied equally to Islam. A similar list of scholars, both Western and Muslim, who have investigated Islam can be presented: Ernest Renan, Friedrich Muller, Julius

Wellhausen, Robertson Smith, Sale, al-Warraq, Ibn al-Rawandi, Ali Dashti, and al-Bukhari to name but a few.

Listen to what one of our Western scholars had to say about a basic aspect of Islam, its holy book, the Koran. Salmon Reinach, a first-rank French investigator, wrote in his classic *Orpheus: A History of Religion*: "From the literary point of view, the Koran has little merit. Declamation, repetition, puerility, a lack of logic and coherence strike the reader at every turn. It is humiliating to the human intellect to think that this mediocre literature has been the subject of innumerable commentaries, and that millions of men are still wasting time in absorbing it."

This is in utter contradiction to the Muslim claim that the miracle of the Koran consists of such an inimitable style and eloquence that it vouchsafes Muhammad's claim to prophethood.

In case you think that Reinach was prejudiced against the Muslims, here's his succinct analysis of the Pauline letters in the New Testament: "The four great Epistles, to the Romans, the Corinthians (1 and 2), and to the Galatians are the most important monuments of that Pauline doctrine which the Apostle himself, quoting the Greeks, called the 'foolishness' of the Cross. They are difficult texts, so rugged in style and capricious in composition, that they make us wonder how the recipients can have understood them. . . . If we read the Epistles without a commentary, we are in peril of a good deal of lost labor and of ultimate bewilderment."

Criticism of their holy book has shown that the Muslims in too many cases have put their own spin on the Western Bible. For instance, in Muslim tradition the Arabs trace their ancestry back to Abraham through Ishmael. Because Paul in his letter to the Galatians reversed the figures of Isaac and Ishmael, the Muslims make Ishmael rather than Isaac the son that Abraham was commanded to sacrifice.

Can the Koran withstand the same onslaught given the Bible by Western scientific analysis? What of Darwin and the theory of evolution that has dealt such a decisive blow to the biblical account of man and creation? Many Jews and Christians have accepted the results of science and have, accordingly, adjusted their beliefs. So have many Muslims.

No longer can we rely on the so-called truths of the Bible and Koran. No longer should we listen to the blatherings of such ostrichlike thinkers as Salam. If he chooses to live in a compartmentalized world, that is his unreality, not ours. His stand that it is ridiculous to believe that his faith has nothing to do with his science is merely wishful thinking. With his irrational point of view Salam would never receive the Nobel Prize for work in religion if he should choose to do so.

# SECULAR HUMANISM

# 47

# From Religious to Secular Literature: The Founding Fathers of Humanism

Ever wonder why religious writing has taken the back burner to what we call secular literature? Are you aware that religious writing was more dominant, and for a longer time, than secular literature? Why, science is merely an adolescent compared to the maturity of theology. In fact, Thomas Aquinas, one of the Church's greatest sons, proclaimed in the thirteenth century that theology and *not* natural philosophy was the "Queen of the Sciences."

Broadly speaking, before and during the same period as Aquinas, in the twelfth and thirteenth centuries, Christian literary theory revived. This is well illustrated by a poem titled *Sir Gawain and the Green Knight.* In it Celtic myth and the conventions of ancestral romantic narrative were blended with themes from the New Testament.

In the fourteenth century the writing of its foremost poet, Geoffrey Chaucer, although rich in biblical references, moves from simple allegory and biblical paraphrase to more worldly tales. In Langland's apocalyptic *Piers Plowman* simple moral and political allegories are projected from the Gospels and Pauline epistles onto contemporary crises in church and state. Authors urge readers toward direct, personal reading of the Scriptures. This is the time of the famous Wycliffe translation, allowing the common man to read and study the Bible.

During the fifteenth century a reaction set in. Wycliffe's Bible was condemned and it became unfashionable to use the same biblical freedom as in the previous century. A person could actually be arrested for owning a copy of *The Canterbury Tales*! The most notable examples of biblical influence were two plays about saints, *The Conversion of St. Paul* and *The Play of Mary Magdalene.*

The sixteenth century saw more translations of the Bible, these by Tyndale, Coverdale, Rogers, and Taverner. With the Bible so accessible, people could now read it through much as they did other literature. In turn, this led to the success of the King James Version in 1611, regarded by many as the high-water mark of English literary prose. This gave rise to much biblically oriented prose and poetry. Nowhere else has the effect of the Bible on literary language been so all-pervasive. Shakespeare in his *Measure for Measure* critiqued the theology of the Puritans by setting his text from Matthew 7 in a rich context of quotations from Paul's letter to the Romans, such as were often featured in the Puritans' own sermons. In his desire to write the great English epic, classically trained John Milton purposely rejected a plot from Greek and Roman literature as well as from the national myth about King Arthur and instead chose the biblical story of the fall and redemption.

Between 1480 and 1660 more than half of all books printed in England were devoted to theological or ethical subjects, many of them written for the lay public. But after the dismal failure of the Puritan Commonwealth under Oliver Cromwell and the restoration under Charles II (1660), there was a marked turning away from anything that resembled piety in public life and the arts. Accordingly, biblical influence on literature suffered a sharp reversal—biblical subject matter and titles almost disappeared. An exception was Defoe's *Robinson Crusoe* (1719), a progenitor of the modern novel.

Adding fuel to the fire was the advent of science. *The rise of science led to religious skepticism and a critical attack on the scientific reliability of the biblical texts themselves.* Skepticism began as a trickle in works such as Lord Herbert, founder of Deism and author of the pro-Deistic *De Veritate* (*On Truth,* 1623). Coupling this to biblical criticism such as Richard Simon's *Critical History of the Old Testament* and the philosophical writings of John Locke, we find a growing flood of challenges to the authority and relevance of the Bible.

Writers of major influence were Anthony Ashley Shaftesbury (greatly influenced by John Locke), Henry Bolingbroke (*Essays Philosophical and Theological*), who took special delight in discrediting the various church creeds, and later, king of the skeptics, David Hume (*Dialogues Concerning Natural Religion*), Thomas Paine (the highly influential *The Age of Reason*), and Edward Gibbon.

Gibbon's *Decline and Fall of the Roman Empire* (1776–1788) celebrated the reinstitution of Roman as opposed to biblical models and values, as well as the English evolution in literature from an era dominated by Christian and biblical influences to one that was now mostly secular. There you find a scattering of poems inspired by the progress in science, using biblical paraphrases of passages in Job or Psalms in an attempt to show the correspondence of Newton and Scripture. Alexander Pope in his *Universal Prayer* (1737) tried to express a theory of the physical universe and of God compatible with the new astronomy and natural science. And William Broome's *A Paraphrase of Parts of Job* (1720) makes the author of Job sound like a lecturer to the Royal Society!

Our humanist movement originates from a very eminent cast of founding fathers who sparked the transition from religious to secular literature. Many of the authors mentioned in the last three paragraphs were the progenitors of the humanist movement and, as such, should compel us to be familiar with their highly provocative and productive ideas.

# Afterword

I've read that Pope John Paul II thinks Catholicism is the greatest humanist force in today's world. This is a fine example of the kind of creative semantics religion has resorted to from its beginnings. John Paul's and our definition of humanism butt each other like two male steers in heat.

Although he didn't state it, the pope's definition clearly includes God and the supernatural; ours emphatically does not. Secular humanism has no truck with the supernatural or superstition. Being scientifically oriented, secular humanism is focused on this world, not the next. Religion has told so many lies that you couldn't believe its spokespersons even if they told you they were lying!

Secular humanism is completely people-oriented. It's convinced that we'd be better off by ignoring the pie-in-the-sky rewards "guaranteed" by clergy, faith healers, and religious con artists.

It is politically democratic. Its emphasis and demand for constitutional rights—free inquiry topping the list—stems from the bloody and repressive history of Western religions. It's a sad fact that today we are faced by many anti-secularist trends: dogmatic, authoritarian religions; fundamentalist, literalist, and muscular Christianity; rabid and uncompromising Islam; nationalistic Jewish orthodoxy; and the resurrection of the so-called New Age religions.

We deplore the growth of religious groups that foment hatred and religious intolerance. No religious organization must be allowed to impose its biased views about what constitutes proper morality, education, sexual behavior, marriage, divorce, birth control, or abortion—or legislate these private concerns for the rest of us. Our ethics is based on critical analysis.

Secular humanists think those who want to require that creationism be taught in science classrooms are either ignorant, mad, or charlatans, or a combination of these. Instead, we insist that evolution, as well as all other scientific disciplines, be taught.

151

We trust the head rather than the heart. Yet, we uphold the emotional side of life by supporting the arts and humanities in all their glory.

Some of the most noteworthy personalities in history have been secularists and humanists: Lucretius, Epicurus, Spinoza, David Hume, Thomas Paine, Diderot, Mark Twain, John Stuart Mill, Charles Darwin, Thomas Edison, Albert Einstein, Margaret Sanger, H. L. Mencken, Bertrand Russell, Ernest Nagel, Sidney Hook, Walter Kaufmann, Isaac Asimov, B. F. Skinner, and Francis Crick. These and many other notables furnish a brilliant genealogy of our movement. We have much to celebrate, but there is still much to be done. My hope is that this book will, in some small way, inspire all of us to do likewise.